Spiritual
Adventures
in *the* SNOW

Skiing & Snowboarding as Renewal for Your Soul

Dr. Marcia McFee and Rev. Karen Foster

Foreword by Paul Arthur

Walking Together, Finding the Way®
SKYLIGHT PATHS®
PUBLISHING
Woodstock, Vermont

Spiritual Adventures in the Snow:
Skiing and Snowboarding as Renewal for Your Soul

2009 Quality Paperback Edition, First Printing

Library of Congress Cataloging-in-Publication Data
McFee, Marcia, 1962–
   Spiritual adventures in the snow : skiing and snowboarding as renewal for your soul / Marcia McFee and Karen Foster ; foreword by Paul Arthur.—Quality pbk. ed.
      p. cm.
   ISBN-13: 978-1-59473-270-6 (quality pbk.)
   ISBN-10: 1-59473-270-1 (quality pbk.)
   1. Skiers—Religious life. 2. Snowboarders—Religious life. 3. Skis and skiing—Religious aspects. 4. Snowboarding—Religious aspects. I. Foster, Karen, 1960–
II. Title.
   BL625.9.A84M34 2009
   204'.40887969—dc22

                                                                2009031342

10 9 8 7 6 5 4 3 2 1

Manufactured in the United States of America
Cover Design: Jenny Buono
Cover Art: @ Galyna Andrushko—Fotolia

SkyLight Paths Publishing is creating a place where people of different spiritual traditions come together for challenge and inspiration, a place where we can help each other understand the mystery that lies at the heart of our existence.

SkyLight Paths sees both believers and seekers as a community that increasingly transcends traditional boundaries of religion and denomination—people wanting to learn from each other, *walking together, finding the way.*

SkyLight Paths, "Walking Together, Finding the Way" and colophon are trademarks of LongHill Partners, Inc., registered in the U.S. Patent and Trademark Office.

Walking Together, Finding the Way®
Published by SkyLight Paths Publishing
A Division of LongHill Partners, Inc.
Sunset Farm Offices, Route 4, P.O. Box 237
Woodstock, VT 05091
Tel: (802) 457-4000   Fax: (802) 457-4004
www.skylightpaths.com

Contents

Acknowledgments

The writing of this book has itself been a spiritual adventure, and we are grateful for the support we've had in putting it all together. We'd like to thank the team at SkyLight Paths Publishing for giving us the opportunity to write about our favorite spiritual practice and for allowing us to call this entire skiing/riding season "research"! It has afforded us the opportunity to expand our friendships to include some of the most adventurous and inspiring people in the world. We are amazed at their generosity. We are especially grateful for the skillful hand of Marcia Broucek, our editor, who has walked us through this process from start to finish. Marcia B., we *will* get you out on the slopes with us, and we will hear you say, "Woo-hoo!" And finally, to Sherrie, Sue, and Zachary, nothing is better than the joy of being in this oh-so-grand adventure with you.

Foreword

It was a great pleasure to participate by writing the foreword for this book, which celebrates spiritual adventures in the snow, and now to have the joy of sharing it with you. Skiing, snowboarding, and other snow sports offer some life-transforming experiences, and reading this book is a great place to start. Like adding color to a black-and-white film, it will take your ordinary snow adventures and make them extraordinary. The ideas that Marcia and Karen present will wind their way into your spirit and your psyche, and you will find yourself experiencing the outdoors, snow, your body—the whole adventure—on a much deeper level.

Karen, Marcia, and I attend worship in the beautiful Squaw Valley Chapel in Olympic Valley, California, which was built for the 1960 Olympics. We are in awe as we look out the sixteen-foot-high windows that face the mountain I have skied for fifty years. I know they agree with me: we also get to "worship" when we are skiing and riding that very mountain. Spirituality is not just for chapels made by human hands; it also thrives in what many call "church of the trees." Our souls, our spirits, are renewed when we allow ourselves to have fun, push on in the face of the ups and downs of life, open ourselves to the mystery of the beauty of creation, and know ourselves deeply when we tune in to the wisdom inherent in physical challenges.

Much like the other adventurers you will meet in this book, I have had many momentous and varied spiritual adventures in the snow. Perhaps it was my experiences with skiing and spending time amid the breathtaking beauty of snowy mountains that taught me about living a spiritual life, a life in which I never cease to be amazed at the grand diversity and inspiring wonder of the natural world. In the midst of growing up, facing challenges, dealing with grief, and experiencing the exhilaration of coaching, I have been renewed by skiing time and again.

Skiing was an important part of my growing up. I first started skiing with the Boy Scouts and the YMCA. Since I did not have money to buy lift tickets, it was a long time before I went anywhere there was a lift. So I learned to ski in the backcountry. It was with the Boy Scouts that I first learned about climbing skins. Climbing skins are an amazing invention that, when placed on the bottom of downhill skis, allow the skier to hike uphill. We climbed and skied Mt. San Georgino near Los Angeles, a very beautiful and spiritual place. It was so daunting that a few of us thought we would die—talk about a spiritual experience—but it was actually quite fun.

My adventures experiencing the wonder and awe of snow began early in my life. Many years ago, Mammoth Mountain had only a couple of rope tows, and the road in was never plowed. Dave McCoy, who eventually developed Mammoth into what it is now, would take people in a truck with giant back wheels up to the ski area. It worked fine until the winter of 1952, when it snowed so much you couldn't get up there. I was staying there that weekend in Ol' Mammoth Tavern. The only way to get out with all that snow was a third-story attic window. The snow was thirty-five feet deep. I was sixteen and helped lead fifty-three folks out from Mammoth to Bishop, a distance of twenty-six miles. We were traversing places where we were on top of forty feet of snow. I had to get out because I had to go to school!

As you'll hear throughout this book, adventures in the snow can offer life lessons—both through the exhilaration of a wonderful day and through facing our difficulties and fears on and off the slopes. I've been in many treacherous situations while ski mountaineering. I was nineteen years old when I was the first to summit and ski down Mt. Whitney, the highest mountain in California. We considered skiing the east side, but it was too narrow to make turns on skis—one turn could pop you off the side, and it's kind of a long fall! We were determined to make it, to stay on snow along the ridgeline. I probably never prayed to survive, but the spiritual feeling and the spiritual contact was definitely there in the focus. I don't think I ever prayed, "God help me have strength to do this," but I thought about it afterward, praying, "Thank you, God, for helping me do it!"

We had U.S. Army–issue sleeping bags and canvas tents and U.S. Army–issue white skis with holes in the tips. With wind chill, it was minus thirty-five to forty degrees in our campout. The difficulty is in battling your mind and body against the weather, going to great lengths to stay alive and keep your spirit up. Challenges were many—little sleep, freezing cold with winds blowing your tent away, desperate to keep your boots warm by tucking them under your armpits or cradling them on your belly during the night, avalanche concerns. After all that, it was worth it. Once you get started skiing, you make it happen. It's like renewing your spirit with each run down a new mountain.

At times, the solace I found during my skiing adventures gave me the strength to endure some of life's greatest difficulties. When my first wife was very sick, I used to go off and ski. One time I skied from Boreal Ridge to Mammoth. I was in the snow for fifteen days, skiing some two hundred miles. Skiing was the only thing that could help me clear my head enough to get me through that difficult time. Another poignant experience involved a friend who died attempting to be the first to accomplish a winter climb of the Eiger in the Bernese Alps. I was supposed to be on that trip with him. A large chunk of ice or rock hit his rope, knocking it loose, and he perished. I was asked to go there and leave a memento of remembrance, which I did in May of 2007. Incredibly, I skied right up against the wall of the Eiger—it's twice as big as El Capitan in Yosemite.

I've also been in three avalanches, and they are no fun. I was buried and thrown completely into the black and then thrown back out. The slide started on the west face of K2 at Squaw Valley, and I was taken down across the large flat expanse of Times Square, down into Squaw Creek, and back up the other side. Its roar was unbelievable; the back of it was going eighty to ninety miles an hour. All the while I was tumbling, I was thinking, "Live!" "Stay on top!" I lost a ski pole and had a sore right ankle. Found my life when I saw sky. Found the pole in June.

As many of the adventurers in this book would say, skiing has given me some of the greatest gifts in my life. One of the accomplishments of which I am most proud is coaching. Envision going to the Junior Olympics with fifty pairs of skis, a bunch of great little hyped-up kids, and a slew of parents, some of whom just get in the way. Imagine waxing all those skis at six in the morning. I found coaching to be personally gratifying, but more important, it was formative for the kids. They had no idea what they were going to achieve—and some of them would find the highest honors in skiing later in life. Their team spirit and their ability to help each other led them to bring home twelve of sixteen trophies at the 1979 Junior Olympics at Crystal Mountain, Washington, leaving only four for the balance of the country. I attribute much of our success to how fun we made it for the kids. We would finish our races and get out and play and have a raucous run down the hill. We would have fifty other kids following our ten because we were having so much fun. These memories can never be erased for them or for me because, as Marcia and Karen suggest, having fun and finding joy nurture the human spirit and heighten our passion for life.

I spend part of the year in Squaw Valley and the other part in Hawaii. I write this as I prepare to go off to Little Hawaii to help our group, Sustainable Kohala, participate in the Earth Day celebration. My spirituality starts with and is grounded in the *aina* (earth). As each day unfolds, I praise God for letting me continue to share the joys of what naturally comes from the world around me. Today at dawn, the saffron finches and cardinals were singing at our newly filled feeders; the sky was a foreboding gray, due to a Kona wind bringing *vog* (volcanic ash–causing smog) from the erupting volcano. All was at peace, with no sounds of people to break the silence, and even with the foreboding gray sky, the spirit of the day was positive. That peace in each day, whether it is on a snowy mountaintop or here in the tropics, is my spirituality, and it can be richly enhanced by sharing it with other people if they are open to the real joy of this earth. As Karen and Marcia share their commitment to the connection between spirituality, community, and love for the earth and its peoples, I hope you, too, will feel the interrelationship of all things.

Finally, on behalf of Marcia and Karen, I am pleased to remember and honor Shane McConkey, Truckee/Tahoe local and internationally renowned big mountain freeskier and BASE jumper.*

Once in Europe, while I was skiing the Monch, Shane was dropped by helicopter on the neighboring summit of the Eiger, a half mile away. He was jumping off while I was skiing down, and I skied right to his tracks where he had landed. Marcia and Karen had hoped to interview Shane for this book, but sadly, he died during the time it was being written. He exemplified the spirit of flight, both in the air and on the snow. He was an inspiration to many and a good friend to all who knew him. I had the privilege to be his first coach, and he is greatly missed.

May spiritual adventures in the snow renew your soul.

Paul Arthur

---

*The acronym BASE stands for Building, Antennae, Span, Earth. BASE jumpers jump from these fixed locations and then parachute to the earth below. Shane innovated the sport of BASE skiing.

Introduction

This book is your invitation to become a spiritual adventurer in the snow. Whether you are an athlete or a novice, whether you have a religious affiliation or not, we want to plant within you an idea that engaging in winter sports can become an experience that renews your soul and opens a connection to something bigger than meets the eye. Both of us grew up in places flatter than a pancake and hotter than blue blazes, but along the way we discovered "altitude"—the natural high of feeling on top of the world in white bliss! Though each of us has theological degrees, we know you don't have to be a trained theologian, or even consider yourself "religious," to become a sage of wonder in the snow.

What Is This Book About?

Spiritual adventurers ourselves, we have the distinct pleasure of living at sixty-five hundred feet and within fifteen minutes of the ski slopes. On one of those crystal-clear blue-sky Tahoe days when the sun glints blindingly on two feet of fresh powder that's fallen overnight, the mountain teems with three kinds of people: professional ski industry folks, who are out there every day, catching moments to breathe deeply, sighing and thanking the universe for their lucky lot in life; vacationers, who zip and zag, or tumble and fall, with smiles as wide as the white terrain; and local mountain dwellers who have called in "sick" to work in order to make fresh tracks. This is what we call a "powder day," and we believe in our bones it's as close to heaven as you can get.

In fact, no matter what word you use to describe nirvana, skiers and snowboarders tend to conjure up language that sounds positively awestruck ... because we are. Whether what bowls you over is the grandeur of rock faces or the delicacy of snowflakes, there is something sacred about these outdoor cathedrals of winter. This book is about articulating and affirming what adventurers in the snow already sense about the spiritual opportunities of the alpine life. And it is a way for novices to discover a deeper experience, to turn mere recreation into spiritual epiphany.

Spiritual Adventures in the Snow: Skiing and Snowboarding as Renewal for Your Soul explores spirituality as something that is fed by play, challenge, physicality, flow, attentiveness, and the wonder of nature. At its root is our belief that the spiritual is found everywhere and life lessons can be learned in myriad ways. The activities of skiing and snowboarding not only offer a tangible physical experience of the sacred nature of our bodies and the earth, but they also provide a rich set of metaphors for seeing life's ups and downs as part of a sacred rhythm.

Each year millions of people like you head for the mountains seeking fun, relaxation, exhilaration, escape, and community. This book adds to that list a search for the renewal of spirit that comes with not only tuning up the ski and snowboard equipment, but also tuning in to the sacred rhythms of gliding down the mountain, sliding over cross country terrain, or snowshoeing in the hush of a moonlit night.

Is This Book for Me?

Spirituality is defined in many ways these days, and we explore many different aspects of that term in this book. Reflection for growing, experiencing oneness with the natural world, connection to others and to something bigger than all of us, depth of wisdom, reconnecting body, mind, and spirit—all of these are expressions of what it means to dive into a spiritual adventure.

We are both in ministry, based in the Christian tradition; however, we believe that there is a vocabulary that cuts across religious boundaries that can help people have common conversations. This is the vocabulary we have chosen to use. We encourage you to use your imagination and the words from your own religious or spiritual tradition, if you have one, to translate where our words don't seem adequate for you.

We have found that people who engage in winter adventures have a common bond of that "oh-so-amazingly-spiritual-but-hard-to-put-into-words" feeling. We try to honor that by putting words to that feeling, as well as opening the way for conversation that is inclusive of people's varied spiritual affiliations. When it is difficult to put something into words, the next best thing to silence is to bring different vocabularies together with openness and generosity in an attempt to communicate what that feeling is.

There is a little something for everyone in this book. If you like stories, you'll find those here. If interesting theories that help explain the body-mind-spirit connection are fun for you, there's some of that, too. If you'd like to know a little more about the "behind-the-scenes" action at a ski resort, you'll find a little of that. And there are practical tips and encouragement about how to extend your adventure into humanitarian projects and environmental responsibility, because we believe that the privilege of engaging in winter adventures, and the heightened consciousness that a spiritual journey creates, lead us to offer our energies and resources to build a better world.

As you read, you will quickly see that we both have a particular affinity for the downhill versions of snow-filled spiritual adventures, but the ideas in this book are applicable to cross country skiing and snowshoeing. Additionally, we know that there is great diversity when it comes to what *kind* of adventures resonate for each of us. Karen has a need for speed on a snowboard, and Marcia's yearning leans more toward lyrical S curves on skis. We've included various perspectives, from novices to world champions, from backcountry enthusiasts to grooming experts, as well as other adventurers with diverse spiritual and religious perspectives. Chances are you'll find yourself somewhere in one or more of these adventures.

If this appeals to you, this book is for you. After you've had some adventures in the snow and discovered more ways to sense the spiritual, you can share your experiences with others. Go to our website, www.spiritualadventuresinthesnow.com, and become part of the Spiritual Adventurers community, inspiring others and being inspired to get out there in the snow.

What's in This Book, and How Do I Use It?

There is no "right" way to read this book—no rules about where to start or what order to read it in. Pick what tickles your fancy or read from front to back if you want. Read it before your adventures in the snow, on the plane as you travel, or a little each night as you soak your tired muscles. Use "A Week of Meditations for Spiritual Adventures in the Snow" at the back of the book to create a weeklong spiritual adventure retreat for yourself. If you are lucky enough to be a local in the mountains, read the book, and then put it in the guest bedroom for all those friends and family members who never visited you before you moved to the mountains!

We have written this book from our own perspectives. In other words, when you read "I ...," the person who is talking is either Marcia or Karen, depending on the chapter. Here is a synopsis of what you'll find as you embark on *Spiritual Adventures in the Snow*:

- Among our favorite features of the book are the "Conversations with an Adventurer" at the end of each chapter. The people we interviewed for these conversations include renowned adventurers and spiritual teachers, all of whom are passionate about snow sports. Each one brings inspirational perspectives to the spiritual aspects of skiing and riding.

- In chapter 1, "Woo-Hoo! Who Said Fun Isn't Spiritual? Adventures in the Snow," Marcia overturns the idea that spiritual pursuits and fun don't mix. She invites you to see adventure as spiritual when you open to its elements of amusement, passion, joy, and play.

- Marcia continues in chapter 2, "Are You Out of Your Mind? The Physicality of Spirituality," debunking the myth that your body has nothing to do with your spirituality. When you can overcome the split between these, you can appreciate the physicality of your adventures in the snow as entry points to renewing your soul.

- Karen takes over in chapter 3, "I Could Kiss the Mountain: Getting Stoked on a Natural High," exploring what it is about being out in nature's playground that opens the possibility for "mountaintop" spiritual experiences.

- Chapter 4, "Freezing Your Fanny Can Be Spiritual? Opportunities of the Winter Season," has Karen reflecting on winter as a particularly poignant time for spiritual nurture and the amazingly unique opportunities afforded by winter darkness, cold, and snow.

- In chapter 5, "Zapped into the Zone: Finding Your Kinesthetic Groove," Marcia explores the "Zone" that athletes strive for in optimal performance—a feeling of "time-out-of-time"—and invites you to embrace your particular rhythms to find your groove for a peak spiritual life.

- Marcia focuses chapter 6, "More Than Buckling Up: Tuning Awareness beyond the Technical," on what is, for spiritual adventurers, as essential as equipment—tuning in and dialing up your presence, intention, and courage.

- Chapter 7, "On My Butt Again: Life Lessons from the Mountain," is Karen's take on the spiritual lessons that derive from the many opportunities for calamity, struggle, and triumph inherent in undertaking challenging physical endeavors in the snow.
- In Chapter 8, "Making a Difference: Putting Spirituality into Action for the Planet and Its Peoples," Karen suggests ways to meld your passion for play in the snow into creative humanitarian efforts and environmental responsibility. The ski/snowboard industry is full of Olympians, professionals, and "regular" people who are doing important work to change the world in positive ways, and she wants you to know about them and be inspired to help.
- Next, we offer "A Week of Meditations for Spiritual Adventures in the Snow." These are based on some of the themes of the chapters and can be used as guides to personal reflection during your adventures.
- At the close of the book, we've given you a must-read glossary titled "How to Talk Cool on the Mountain: A Guide to Slope Slang." Refer to it if you encounter terms in the book you've never heard before, but also be sure to read it in its entirety. It will tickle your funny bone and help you be a snow tourist without looking and sounding like one!

Our two families moved to the Tahoe region to live year-round about the same time a few years ago. We have a favorite exclamation that wells up in moments when the pleasure and privilege of living in this majestic winter wonderland overtakes us: "We *live* here!" It is our hope that you, too, will have the opportunity to find exuberant renewal for your soul in high elevations and discover for the first time, or once again, that adventures in the snow can be deeply spiritual.

1

Woo-Hoo! Who Said Fun Isn't Spiritual?

Adventures in the Snow

THOUGHTS FROM MARCIA

"SPIRITUAL ... ADVENTURES?" When you picked up this book, your mind may have done a double take. Our brains tend to do this when two things that seem unlikely companions are presented side by side. When you saw the word "spiritual," you may have conjured up sedate images of meditation, prayer, quiet reflection, a disciplined form of reading or study, or perhaps stereotypical angelic choir music. And then here came the word "adventures." Screeech! goes the soundtrack in your brain, and the cherub choir starts falling off their pedestals, halos askew and harp strings bursting. Perhaps images of adventure reside in the part of your brain that thinks of X-Games-like escapades or pushing into the unknown. Adventure for you may be about trying something new, attempting something you never imagined you would do. The particular folder in your brain where you file "adventure" may be where you would put your memories of sports and recreation in the snow. But *spiritual* adventures in the snow?

Karen and I would like to explore the possibility that "spiritual" and "adventure" can happen in the same experience. We're not suggesting that this drastically changes the images you already have about what it means to be on a ski or snowboarding adventure. Rather, we think that adventure *is* already spiritual and that our souls—that which gives depth to our experience— can be renewed through various kinds of escapades. It may be that we just need to rethink our definitions of both "adventure" and "spirituality," opening the possibility that adventures can carve deeper spaces for the soul, understanding that spirituality can be, in a word, *fun*. In fact, fun may be one of the most neglected spiritual practices of our stressful time.

Facts about stress show that an overwhelming majority of people experience stress on a regular basis—and not the good kind of stress that raises our adrenaline levels and helps us have more energy when we need it. We're talking about the unhealthy kind of stress, which produces the same physical effects of elevated adrenaline and other chemicals but for extended periods of time. Our bodies start out thinking they need these to survive the current tense moment, but if kept at a high level for too long without an outlet or any relief, these chemicals can produce all kinds of negative effects. When these tense moments turn into days and weeks, our bodies begin to break down our ability to cope, which in turn begins to affect our work and our relationships. Essentially, stress dampens our spirits. It suppresses our joy.

So what is the antidote? We think it includes spending some of that adrenaline on fun on the slopes. The kind of fun that, when combined with wonder and attentiveness to the pleasures and beauty that surround us, can renew us like nothing else. When fun is infused with the intention of renewing our souls, we find ourselves on a spiritual adventure.

We often think of fun activities as things that we work to *deserve* rather than something we have a right to experience: "I work hard so I can play hard." We too rarely think of fun as essential to our health and well-being. We may be influenced in part by messages handed down to us from an era, or even a religious perspective, that considered pleasure and recreation something to be earned or, worse yet, something that could be detrimental to a virtuous life. The philosopher Plato said, "Pleasure is the greatest incentive to evil," and this message has pervaded human society ever since.

Yet this is not the only story promoted by thinkers and theologians. Enjoyment, fun, pleasure, or whatever name you give it, has also long been thought to be a part of what each of us needs for a life lived fully and meaningfully. An ancient proverb says, "They who allow their days to pass by without practicing generosity and enjoying life's pleasures are like a blacksmith's bellows: they breathe but do not live." In other words, living is much more than the mechanics of blowing air in and out, which would make us not much more than "blowhards." To truly live—to breathe deeply the fullness of what it means to be on this earth—is to enjoy the gifts given to us and to share this joy freely with others.

> "Life is not measured by the number of breaths we take, but by the moments that take our breath away."
> —Anonymous

Activities that are exhilarating and fun are not usually thought of as spiritual. But to the contrary, such ventures may well point us to our most profound spiritual connections. For when we are able to come fully into the present moment, turn off the noise in our minds, feel our true essence as complete union of body-mind-spirit, we enter into a kind of "other worldly" state of ecstasy that we can experience only as a spiritual dimension. Add to this the overwhelming beauty of snowy mountains under blue skies, along with the igniting of our passion for motion and rhythm that is part dance and part flight, and we end up with a recipe for a literal and figurative "mountaintop experience."

Are you ready to begin this adventure in rethinking spirituality? We'll start by taking a look at some of the ways our souls are replenished by fun: amusement, joy and passion, and play.

Spiritual Fun as Amusement

When we think of something "amusing," we tend to think of light-hearted fun. A trip to the amusement park releases us into a time of make-believe filled with fanciful characters and wild rides that get our hearts pumping or raise some goosebumps at the back of our necks. This in itself is not a bad way to release tension and let off steam. But if we unlayer the word "amusement," we find something of substance that is essential to renewing our souls. The medieval origin of the word "amusement" comes from the French *amuser*, meaning "to cause to muse." And what did it mean to muse? Well, literally, it meant to "sniff about like a dog"! To muse is to ponder, to stick our noses in something. Curiosity is part of our lives. To be fascinated, to want to discover, to look past what we already know and instead consider what we might learn is to keep renewing our lust for this amazing life.

Pushing ourselves to discover new things on skis or a snowboard is the focus of this book, but take a step back for a moment to the reason we can even get on that equipment: snow. The fluffy white stuff is a great source of amusement. Have you ever been with someone who saw snow for the first time? It may have been someone who grew up in a warm climate or a child discovering winter for the first time. Seeing snow for the first time can be an awe-filled experience. I have a friend from Texas who was so excited the first time she encountered really deep snow that she ran and flung herself down in a bank of snow on her back to make a snow angel. (Unfortunately, it was a bank of snow on the side of the road made by a snowplow several days earlier, and it was so hard-packed that it knocked the wind right out of her!) No matter our age, we turn into kids again with a childlike fascination and wonder at the sight of snow.

I can't remember the first time I saw snow because by six months of age I was living in Alaska. During the first four years of my life, I literally grew up with snow. I have photos of me and my friends in the igloos our fathers made for us, and other photos of my mom pulling me on the sled to the store. But even though I now get to live in Tahoe, and I visit other places where snow falls every year, the sight of it never ceases to create a flutter of excitement in me. Last night I sat in a glass-enclosed porch on a deck overlooking the "lower" range of the Colorado mountains at eighty-five hundred feet, where I was visiting and skiing. The weather forecast called for a late spring snowstorm that had everyone in town buzzing and winter sports enthusiasts in Denver packing up their cars to make the trip to new snow at higher elevations. The storm clouds began rolling over the upper range as the last light of day faded. I had gone inside to do some dishes and watch some television, but just before bedtime, I stepped back out onto the deck and turned on the light. What was revealed made me gasp. I had forgotten that it might start snowing, and here were huge white flakes swirling in ten different directions, blown ferociously by the wind. I sat down in my "observatory" and felt like I was in the middle of a snow globe that someone had just shaken with glee. I'd seen snowstorms thousands of times, but once again this felt like a brand-new experience—a perspective like none other. This was the best show on earth, compliments of an Adventurous Creator, and I felt like I had the best seat.

> "The first fall of snow is not only an event, it is a magical event. You go to bed in one kind of a world and wake up in another quite different, and if this is not enchantment then where is it to be found?"
>
> —J. B. Priestley, English novelist and playwright

It has been said, "God is in the details." Looking out over a mountain range in a snowstorm is one kind of awe, but observing the little things, following the course of a small bit of creation's life, can also offer a way to slow down, notice a different pace of life, and be amused. In fact, another definition of the word "muse" is "to stare fixedly at" something, and that is precisely what we do when we tune in to the mystical part of nature through the seemingly insignificant, and often unnoticed, things.

One of my favorite things to do is to keep watch of one spot, one thing, one tiny detail of creation, over the course of a period of time. Last winter there were three pinecones hanging together on a limb high in one of the pine trees behind my house. I noticed them because, though most of the other pinecones had fallen to the ground in the fall, they refused to let go. So I decided to keep watch during the winter, taking pictures from various angles throughout their season of hanging on. Sometimes they were so weighted down with heavy snow I could barely see them. I would wake each morning with anticipation, wondering whether the weight of more snow had pushed even one of them to the ground below. But there they were, every morning, snow-covered spheres valiantly suspended two stories high. It wasn't until the next fall that they succumbed to gravity and the life cycle of the tree and other creatures. The next phase of their journey was to become sustenance, as squirrels decimated them into piles of hulls and ran off fat-cheeked to where they would slowly eat the stash of pine nuts through the next winter.

> "Creativity arises from our ability to see things from many different angles."
> —Keri Smith, *How to Be an Explorer of the World*

Year can pass into year, season into season, if we don't find ways to mark time in meaningful ways. My amusement with three pinecones gave me a marker for that winter. It happened to be a particularly trying time in my life, with lots of stress and worry. But the tenacity of the pinecones, even when weighted down with more than it seemed they could bear, provided me with an image I will never forget, a symbol pointing to a spirit of survival and strength.

We were created to discover, to wonder, to ponder, to learn, and to grow. When we lose our ability to be amused, we lose a bit of our spirit. To go on a spiritual adventure is to become an explorer who lives by the rules of amusement. Going back to the word's origin, those "rules" include sticking your nose in the air like a dog, catching a scent, and following it to see where it leads. Go ahead and be overwhelmed by the vast expanse of the mountains, but also turn your attention to the details. If you are a veteran of fun and exploration in the snow, challenge yourself to renew your sense of amusement. Take notice of what's around you. A particular tree, for example, might catch your eye. Instead of looking past it, notice it some more. What is there that you didn't see at first glance? Look at it from a different angle to discover something new about it, to get a different perspective. Consider that this tree, any tree, *everything* could hold a clue to an "aha" moment, a new perspective. Or—and this is just as valid—it could just be light-hearted fun for the moment, a moment of freedom from stressors, like my snow globe experience during a late spring Colorado storm. And that's enough to claim it as renewal for your soul.

Spiritual Fun as Joy and Passion

One of my favorite sounds on the slopes is "woo-hoo!" as someone is overcome with the thrill of the moment and their passion *has* to find an outlet. The wide-open outdoors may be one of the few places where we feel we can let out our inner howl. Most of our lives we are cautioned not to exceed the limits of moderate behavior. "Don't be too loud or boisterous." "Don't act too excited over something." "Talk with your 'inside voice.'" But getting outside can allow us to let go of primordial urges to let out a good "whoop and holler," as they say where I grew up in the Midwest. And somehow this is rather common and completely acceptable when skiing or snowboarding. In fact, a spontaneous "woo-hoo" often attracts other yelps echoing in agreement across the mountain.

Skiing and riding elicit passion like nothing else for many people. This passion compels some people to drive in bumper-to-bumper traffic every weekend in the winter just to get a few hours on the mountain trails. It can get even a teenager up in the wee hours of the morning to hit the slopes as soon as they open. For some, this passion means eschewing conventional jobs or home life to be able to follow the snow in whatever hemisphere it happens to be falling. All this just to capture the "woo-hoo" feeling. In fact, the reasons for all this intensity are at times difficult to put into words, so "woo-hoo" is one of the ways we can find to express the joy.

Spiritual adventures involve plugging into our passion and joy. When we allow something to take root in us as a burning desire and then honor it by following that bliss, we also give a gift to the world. How so? Because people who are plugged into their passion are able to tap into an invaluable resource of energy and love for creating joy in the world. I have found that local ski and snowboard communities are filled with people who have a joy and passion that are contagious. Their common love of snow sports strengthens and builds the bonds of community.

> "It doesn't happen all that often. In fact, when it does happen you usually remember it for a long time afterwards. You're skiing down a hill and a supreme happiness overcomes you."
>
> —Alex West, *The Weekly* magazine of North Tahoe

Recently, I sat writing in the local coffee hangout in Truckee, California, called Wild Cherries, run by former Olympian Kristin Krone. The place was crawling with young people looking like someone had put Wite-Out on their faces, just around their eyes down to their cheekbones. It was the day after the legendary Tahoe mountain resort Squaw Valley had closed for the season. No doubt this crowd had spent the day before finding whatever snow was left on a gorgeous sunny spring day (hence the sunburns that left "raccoon eyes" where their goggles had been).

On this day they were talking about "what's next." Some were heading to South America for the Southern Hemisphere winter, and some were already talking about the surf season just three hours away on the coast of California. Such are the migration patterns of those whose passion for the slopes—and often boards in general (whether on snow or water)—calls them to this vocation of adventure. Many are entrepreneurs who use the very best creativity to make these journeys of following their passions, whatever the cost.

Tim Konrad, the founder of an "unofficial" website connecting those who ski and ride at Squaw Valley, sat in the corner with his computer, no doubt adding another blog report to his site and making plans for next season. As we talked that day, Tim told me that his first ride at Squaw Valley Resort was on an Easter morning. He was feeling guilty for not being at church. The cable car heading up the mountain was packed with people when somebody spoke his very thought: "I feel bad that I'm not at church on Easter." Then someone else shouted, "Hey, I *am* on the way to church!" and appreciative yelps from the crowd followed. It has stuck with him ever since. The connection to something spiritual about snow sports, and the feeling that this is a passionate, soul-full adventure to those who seek it out, characterize Tim's excitement about what he does. He wrote in his blog:

> "Like a really great taco or a knee-buckling kiss or a full moon on a clear night, when joy appears in your cup ... stick in your straw and maybe another straw for a buddy. And together, suck it up."
>
> —Howard Hanger, *Drink Deeply with Delight*

When I asked my friend George, who is heading back to the States this week, what he will remember most about his month in Las Lenas [Argentina], he said that more than anything he will remember the amount of stoke and excitement on the faces of his fellow riders. As much fun as the powder skiing has been over the past month, what really ends up counting is your knowledge that you were blessed with a moment in time that will never be forgotten. Events like this would mean nothing if you could not share it with like-minded people who are as excited for you as you are for them.... Skiing is more than a sport to us. Skiing is a way of life and life is good.

Bloggers like Tim are the voice of a culture, the ones who provide a digital connection to a community that thrives on banter about everything snow. They are, I believe, the unofficial priests of what is "church-of-the-mountains" for so many. I say "priest" here not in the typical religious sense, but in the word's root meaning as "bridge builder." They are the bridges for people skiing and riding all over the world. They help bridge the chasm between experiences and stories of those experiences. They name moments, offer ways to mark the what-happens-here of this adventure-loving "congregation."

"For you shall go out in joy, and be led back in peace; the mountains and the hills before you shall burst into song, and all the trees of the field shall clap their hands."

—Isaiah 55:12

On the last day of the season, Tim wrote, "The season was full of strikes and gutters, ups and downs. We experienced plenty of smiles, laughter and high fives but also sad nights and missed loved ones." He was undoubtedly referring to the death of Shane McConkey, beloved Tahoe local freeskier and innovator who died that season BASE jumping in Italy. Hundreds showed up for the memorial gathering at Squaw Valley Resort because Shane's life had touched so many. But it was this coming together of a community that ignited a renewed sense of joy, partially because we were reminded of the strong bonds that exist between us. In the days after Shane's death, a website was established to coordinate meals for Shane's wife and young daughter, and also to offer a place for the community to leave supportive messages and express grief. The man who had been known as "an eternal jokester" and "thought provoker" brought a legacy of joy and deep passion to a community that turned its grief into celebration of a life well lived.

Recapturing joy in the midst of the toughest of times is something that ancient spiritual writers saw as essential. Psalms of lament in the Hebrew biblical texts, written during a time of exile and hardship, are gut-wrenching: "My tears have been my food day and night" (Psalm 42:3). Yet the writers turn to praise in these psalms, seemingly in spite of themselves: "Why are you cast down, O my soul?... Hope in God, for I shall again praise [God]!" (Psalm 42:5). In reclaiming the sense that we are not alone and that hope resides even in the worst of times, there is renewed joy and energy for taking steps forward.

❋ A *Reflective Moment*

When you take time to break from the "same ol', same ol'," and take a wider view of creation (and the mountains are an incredible place for this to happen), you might discover that to be "spiritual" is to sense and create a connection to a passion within you, as well as a connection to others that is deep and lasting. What connections would you like to make? What would you have the energy to do if your spiritual well of joy and passion were filled by this adventure? Do you feel as if you spend most of your time "just making it," just getting by in your small corner of the world, without enough time to nurture relationships beyond the superficial or to follow a passionate dream? Imagine what "going out with joy" from your time in the mountains and hills could mean to your ability to make a positive impact. Imagine the echoes of your enthusiastic "woo-hoo" on the slopes resounding past the peaks to the rest of your life, even and especially if parts of that life seem depleted of joy. Make a commitment to stir the holy fire of passion within you, let out a yelp, and head out with an ear-to-ear grin on your face.

Spiritual Fun as Play

So, who says fun isn't spiritual and play isn't meant for adults? Well, plenty of people do, actually. Unfortunately, we tend to put things into boxes or set up things in opposition to each other, such as "child is to adult as play is to work." But to place things in dichotomies or on opposite poles is to rob us of the wonderful richness and complexity of life. Nothing could be further from the truth—at least the spiritually nourishing truth—than the idea that adults no longer need to play. We encourage play in children because we know it enhances their growth as human beings. They learn to be curious, to discover, to adapt, to cooperate, and to create—not to mention mature mentally and emotionally. Honestly, I can't think of one adult who doesn't need to keep honing these things. Can you?

> "Joy is the holy fire that keeps our purpose warm and our intelligence aglow."
> —Helen Keller, deaf-blind author and political activist

Play can be described as "fooling around." This is an important translation. It means we can come at things with a willingness to engage in something where an end product is not the primary focus. It means we get to live with fewer expectations for just a while. *Whew.* What a relief! The spirit of play can be powerful. To be okay with risking looking like a fool, to live with fewer expectations, is to free ourselves from things that put us on the defensive. When we can be less afraid of failure, we can be more open to possibility.

Interestingly, it is usually our own expectations that are the most difficult to let go of. If your first adventures in skiing or snowboarding carry the expectation that you will be whizzing down the mountain immediately, feeling free as a bird, then you are setting yourself up for frustration. These are the people who, when I ask them if they ski, say, "Oh, I tried that, and after falling on my butt all morning, I just gave up and went to the lodge."

> "Be not afraid of life. Believe that life is worth living and your belief will help create the fact."
> —William James, nineteenth-century psychologist and philosopher

Play is a decision to delight in whatever comes our way, even if that means falling again and again. I asked a friend what kept her going back time after time the first year she was learning to snowboard (which usually means learning the fine art of falling and getting up). Her answer was "the environment I was in. I'd look around and see where I was and just grin from ear to ear. I wanted to get to the top of the mountain so badly, and I knew the only way I could go there was to have a snowboard strapped onto my feet and the ability to make it back down." The magic of that possible moment outweighed any misery. Delight and desire combined to keep her trekking back to the bunny slope over and over until she was standing up and carving turns from high on the peak.

We often call skiing and snowboarding "sports," and they are. It is a rush to watch some of the most amazing athletes at the top of their physical stamina, astounding grace, and acrobatic flair achieving faster, longer, higher, and more daring feats. But even those who train these athletes will tell you that if there is no play, no fun, no pleasure in

> "I'm fanatical about sport: there seems to me something almost religious about the fact that human beings can organize play, the spirit of play."
> —Simon Gray, British playwright, author, and lecturer

the pursuit, the athletes with the most physical prowess will not be the champions. "We discover that games of all kinds are more often won when first they are enjoyed," says Olympic "mental" coach Robert Kriegel. In the midst of the hard work that it takes to be a world-class athlete, there has to be a love for "playing" the sport.

Just as "adult" and "play" are not opposites, neither are "work" and "play." In learning a new snow sport, we know we're going to have to work to get better at our technique. As beginners we work at playing—standing on a snowboard a few minutes longer, getting a smoother skate, or making "French fries" with the skis instead of plowing in the shape of a "pizza." But if we infuse that "work" with a delight in the process, even a few seconds of the "whee" feeling will

> "My, how time flies when you're having fun!"
> —Anonymous

have been worth the effort. Many ski and snowboard instructors create games for their group lessons to free learners' minds from self-consciousness so they can relax, concentrating on the game rather than their technique. Reports show that when adult students engage in games, they often recapture the essence of childlike play and end up learning more quickly and having more fun.

If we can see the connection between work and play in our adventures, then perhaps we can translate those connections back into our jobs. How often is getting to the outcome, meeting the deadline, fulfilling expectations, or "winning" the deal or promotion the thing that ends up overwhelming us in our jobs and everyday lives? We sacrifice delight in the process so much so that sometimes we forget how to capture delight even while we are "playing." From a spiritual view, play is not only a way to "let our hair down" occasionally but also an essential practice in keeping a balance in our lives. Just as a winter athlete must never lose the sense of the thrill of the sport itself, so too does renewing our spirit through our adventures—remembering to truly play—become high on the list of priorities when it comes to a life enjoyed thoroughly and soulfully on and off the slopes.

Time has become such a commodity. We measure it, charge for it, schedule it, parse it out, and too often bemoan the fact that there are only twenty-four hours in a day. We try to squeeze every ounce of productivity out of a period of time and feel proud of our ability to multitask, eking the most out of our "precious time." To have an adventure is to embrace a bit of the unknown. To do this requires letting go of plans, expectations, and preconceived ideas about what will happen.

Sometimes when I'm skiing at a new mountain (well, what I mean is a ski resort that is unfamiliar to me … a "new" mountain would be an oxymoron), I can spend so much time looking at the map and trying to be on the right trails, in order to get the most out of the mountain, that I suck the fun right out of the skiing. Although it is advisable to have a good idea of where you are going (so you don't get on a lift that lands you in terrain that's going to freak you out completely— unless you're an expert), once you know you are heading for a general area that can accommo-

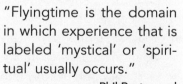

"Flyingtime is the domain in which experience that is labeled 'mystical' or 'spiritual' usually occurs."
—Phil Porter and Cynthia Winton-Henry, founders of InterPlay

date your skill level, there's got to be more than just looking for the next trail sign. I can always tell when I'm really in need of some letting-go-ness in my life when I can't shake my anxiety about finding my way around. It's then that I realize I'm missing the journey because I'm worrying so much about the destination.

"Flyingtime" is what my friends (and experts on play) Phil Porter and Cynthia Winton-Henry call letting go into play. When we're lost in the spirit of play, we stop counting hours and minutes and enter an expanded sense of the present. When we don't have every moment planned and choreographed, we get to improvise.

We get to make choices based on what catches our fancy in the moment. When we experience something and we want more of it … okay, why not? We can stay with it. We do that particular run again. We stop and savor a view a little longer. We come out of a forest trail to see a perfectly smooth open space, and for no reason in particular and without having planned it, we decide to make a big peace sign by tromping about in our snowshoes.

> "Enjoy life. This is not a dress rehearsal."
>
> —Anonymous

Without occasional periods in our life when this kind of play is possible, our spirits suffer under a suffocating regime of conformity—even if it is self-imposed. What comes to your mind when you hear the phrase, "I had the time of my life!"? I would venture a guess that your answer has very little to do with your appointment book. The "Adventure Rabbi" Jamie Korngold (see the "Conversation with an Adventurer" at the end of chapter 4), who leads people on spiritual skiing trips, says, "I am such a non-fan of counting vertical or counting runs. I just really caution people to stay away from that and not make the day into a race." Counting and measuring our own accomplishments or comparing our "statistics" to that of others can pull us right into the rat race of "measuring up" that so much of everyday life asks of us.

The spirit of adventure invites us to "the time of our lives," time that is soul filling and not depleting. A time-out-of-time where imagination takes the lead and surprise is the reward. A time of play that rekindles our joy and the hope for new possibilities. A time when we feel renewed passion that ignites our courage to expand our energies into the world. Come on along! Plunge into spiritual adventure!

Conversation with an Adventurer
Anne Lamott, author and exuberant novice

~

Anne Lamott is the best-selling author of *Traveling Mercies*, *Plan B*, and *Grace (Eventually): Thoughts on Faith*, along with several novels and other works of nonfiction. A spiritual activist for peace and justice, she also relishes being a mom. Anne understands that being able to laugh at ourselves is one of the noblest of spiritual practices and that spirituality does not run counter to fun, laughter, and looking foolish. Here, she offers her perspective of being a spiritual adventurer in the snow.

Do you find skiing to be a spiritual experience?

The way I personally ski down the mountains is intensely spiritual because I am seriously incompetent and therefore must trust in the process of letting go and surrendering. I also trust the inner skier, who knows enough basics to survive (albeit with bruises and occasional mortification), where if I trust my mind, it is like believing in the meanest, craziest relative or teacher you've ever known. I hum hymns on the way downhill—"Blest Be the Ties That Bind" is my favorite skiing hymn for some reason, along with "Softly and Tenderly." I also say my mantra, *"Hari Om Tatsat, Jai Guru Datta,"* and put all together, I have never been seriously hurt. Once I nearly was—I could have truly wiped out, in a major and catastrophic way—and when I didn't, I was able to believe *way* more deeply that, in life and death and on the slopes, I am God's.

What is it about snow that helps you connect in a spiritual way?

The snow is *so* profound—stunningly beautiful, destructive, revealing of the shapes and outlines of the mountains and trees it covers, radiating life and reflecting the sun and creating magical mystical scapes, yet at the same time obliterating from view so much of the land, providing so much joy and wonder; causing so much grief and damage; so hilariously hard to walk in, instantly making everyone seem clumsy and clunky, like we really are; yet powder-smooth so that good skiers look like angels, like gods. So, in short, I think it shows all the complex ways we and life really are.

What do you think it is about skiing that lends itself to being a spiritual adventure?

The most profound spiritual experience of all is being kind to yourself while you are flailing and falling on your butt for all to see. It's a chance to live through everyone's worst elementary school nightmare, of being exposed in front of the cool kids. But when you fall on a slope, it turns out to be an innocent mistake, and the others don't mock or ostracize you. They stop to make sure you're okay, and they help you get upright, and start over again from scratch—with the blessing of their kindness on you.

What life lessons are to be learned from this kind of experience?

It teaches you that it's okay to appear ridiculous when you're trying to do something exhilarating and hard. It teaches you that you get to keep starting over and over again as you make your way down that staggeringly beautiful mountain. It gives you the gift of seeing your own vulnerability and heroism. Of course, we all wish we would look like that great Olympian Picabo Street, but of course most of us look more like the lovable French film dimwit Mr. Hulot, with his hilarious sidesteps and cluelessness. But miraculously, that doesn't keep us from getting to do it along with everyone else. It's the opposite of being so different and feeling like such a loser in junior high, when funky hair or teeth or height meant you didn't get to *belong*. On the mountain, everyone's trying their best, making progress, failing, falling, clumsily getting up or being helped by a stranger, and just dusting the snow off one another and starting out again. Even if you're on a bunny slope, you're part of the oneness, part of a majestic Whole, like being one person in the living organism of a peace march or a soup kitchen. One mountain white with snow under one sky, and it smells so crazily great and green and clean, of evergreens and powdered rain and joy … and then, God willing, of roaring fires and cocoa and burgers and fries and sweaty, tired, happy people all around who all made it back, together.

2

Are You Out of Your Mind?

The Physicality of Spirituality

THOUGHTS FROM MARCIA

"ARE YOU OUT OF YOUR MIND?"

We're not referring to a phrase some of you might have exclaimed the first time you were invited on a ski trip. First-timers, especially adults, often conjure up images of leg casts and sore back-ends when faced with the idea of careening down a mountain at breakneck (hopefully not literally) speed. In this chapter, being "out of your mind" refers to honoring the activity of your *body* as part of your spirituality.

Having debunked the theory that fun has nothing to do with spirituality, and hopefully convinced you that fun is actually a valuable part of your spiritual life, we're out to debunk another theory: the one that says that spirituality and physicality (our bodies) have nothing to do with each other. If "spiritual stuff" is something you've relegated to indoor religious services where the most you might do with your body is sit or stand, we want to expand your notion of how we get connected to that Something Bigger Than Just Us. It's all part of the journey to embrace adventures in the snow as thoroughly spiritual.

In the book *Inner Skiing*, sought-after speaker and seminar designer W. Timothy Gallwey and former Olympic coach Robert Kriegel talk about how vitally important it is to trust your body's wisdom. They talk of skiing "out of your mind." The "mind" that they are referring to is The Judge, The Critic, The Voice inside your head that keeps incessantly repeating every little thing you've learned in a lesson—and the voice that tells you how, if you don't follow directions, falling down will hurt! These author/coaches say that if you get that annoying mind chatter to quiet down and let your body do what it already knows how to do (which is an amazing amount), you'll learn much more quickly, and once you've learned, you'll get incredible "wow" experiences more often as you ski or board.

"Gravity is love, and every turn is a leap of faith."
—Anonymous

Today, in one single day, I conquered more difficult slopes than I have ever done in my life. It seemed I ate them up one by one. I would get to a precipice, see angles I never thought I'd slide down, much less ski, grin at them (well, I'm not sure I stopped grinning), and take off. I flew. I soared. It was "one of those days" that keep me coming back time and again to the mountain.

This isn't to say that there weren't a couple of times that I wavered and wobbled, having caught an edge of my ski. In those conditions, I could have totally "bit it," and it would have probably hurt pretty bad. But I didn't. I wavered and wobbled, and my body self-corrected. And I didn't let The Voice say, "Oh, my gosh (or something along those lines), you shouldn't be doing this, this is way beyond you, slow down, get off, are you *crazy*!" Instead, I just calmly noticed that my body, through a series of minute and complex balancing and correcting movements, knew exactly what to do in that split-second instance. I realized that my body knew way more than the analytical, play-by-play Voice in my head could ever know or even say to me in that blip of a moment. And I began to trust my body wisdom just a little bit more.

Technically, I was not skiing "out of my mind" today, as if my mind and body were two different things. Actually, the idea of being "out of our minds" is an oxymoron. No offense to the authors of *Inner Skiing*—I totally get the distinction they are making, and I'm a believer in their coaching methods—but we have lived for so long with the false division of mind and body to the detriment of how it all relates to spirit that I'd like to play with looking at it in a different way.

The mind, or the part of us that "knows" things, is not just the conscious, analytical mind. Nor is it located only in our head. We have a "mind" in our body, too, with its incredibly complex set of feedback systems working in concert with brain functions. There's no way to be out of our minds because our bodies *are* our minds, just as our bodies are also our spirit.

In other words, we're all one entity because there is no way to sense any experience—physical, mental, or spiritual—without our bodies. The experiences of our bodies will have an effect on what we think and feel and how we understand the "sacred" or the "soul." What constitutes the feeling of oneness, of deep joy, or of profound knowing is intimately tied to the experience of our bodies. The wind in our face as we fly down the slope, the sun warming us as we skate cross country, the thrill of our snowboard lifting off the ground are physical entry points to the sense of spiritual essence. There is a constant convening of body, mind, and spirit. The key is to open our awareness to "the physicality of spirituality."

> "Olympism ... exalting and combining in a balanced whole the qualities of body, mind and will."
> —Pierre de Coubertin, French educator primarily responsible for the revival of the Olympic Games in 1894

Body-Mind Split

We have inherited a big whopping problem. For a long time, theories about how we know things—including spiritual things—

came from the belief that the mind is "disembodied." Imagine the comics that have little dialogue bubbles floating above the characters' heads, and you have a picture of what people used to believe about how we think. In this view, thinking happened without input from our bodies; the mind worked independently, having nothing to do with feelings, emotions, perception, or motor capacities. In fact, many believed the body was "up to no good" and could be a distraction from "pure" thought and spiritual pursuits. Messy things happen in relationship to bodies—emotions, desire, sensations. Oh, my!

> "This is my simple religion. There is no need for temples; no need for complicated philosophy. Our own brain, our own heart is our temple; the philosophy is kindness."
> —Tenzin Gyatso, Dalai Lama and winner of the Nobel Peace Prize

The father of rationalism, Socrates, argued that our bodies were part of our "irrational" self and separate from our true soul. A thousand years later philosopher René Descartes took this body-mind separation to the limit, saying that knowledge had nothing to do with the sensing capabilities of our bodies. He created what would have been a great horse cart bumper-sticker slogan in his time: "I think, therefore I am." We exist because we think with our minds, he taught. And anything worth knowing comes by some "out-of-body" thinking mode.

Do you know the classic Rodin sculpture, *The Thinker*, who sits with his chin in his hand contemplating the universe? Thinking is represented in a very still sitting posture that looks more like what you do when constipated. But if you look at this guy more closely, he is physically, muscularly "ripped" as well! Could it be that the thinking man also got mental breakthroughs while racing that horse cart, muscles engaged, wind in his face, scenery flying by?

By the end of the 1800s, the canyon between mind and body was entrenched in the major institutions of learning and religion. "True knowledge" was considered the job of new classes of experts in education, medicine, philosophy, and theology, replacing the experience of bodily knowing long practiced by mystics, shamans, and wise people in various cultures.

I want to be clear about something. The advances by experts in the past two centuries have been nothing short of amazing. But since the advent of neuroscience, we now know that we *need* our bodies to know anything. There is no such thing as a thought without an emotion connected to that thought. All of our discoveries—no matter how intellectual they are or how much empirical research we've done in the pursuit of them—are impossible without the whole system of feelings and bodily sensations. We would simply be overwhelmed with the amount of data in just about every decision of our lives if we didn't have one important shortcut—our *gut feelings* about things. All along, we have had to pay attention to our bodies for our thinking to actually function.

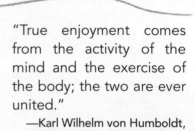

"True enjoyment comes from the activity of the mind and the exercise of the body; the two are ever united."
—Karl Wilhelm von Humboldt, philosopher, educator, and linguist

As skiers and riders, we may already have experienced what research studies are now revealing: when it comes to giving our conceptual powers the best possible advantage, moving our bodies is advantageous. Even something as simple as getting up and taking a stretch break during study (or any work that keeps us in that constipated-looking position at our desks) increases our intellectual productivity by leaps and bounds. Can you imagine what skiing might do for our brain power?

But even more basic than how moving our body helps our brain power is the fact that we now know that thoughts *themselves* are physical. The more we know about the activity of the brain, the more we understand that the brain is not just the gray matter between our ears, but an intricate neural network that runs throughout the body. We know some things only because our feet or hands or any other parts of our bodies are communicating particular sensations throughout the system. How we know things has a lot to do with our "visceral" (gut) experiences. Activity in our intestines may be our first clue about how we are feeling about something. Turns out that "I just had a feeling" is something to pay attention to!

Bottom line: mind and body cannot function separately, and engaging in physical activities such as skiing and snowboarding engages not only the body, but taps into our wisdom as well.

Body-Spirit Split

The problem with the body-mind split didn't stop there. If anything, the body and the "spirit" were seen as even more distant from each other. During the Enlightenment period of the eighteenth and nineteenth centuries, rational thinking was viewed as something higher and more sacred than almost anything. If people could explain something with words, if they could debate it, analyze it, and dissect it, then it was "real." Even spiritual practices among many traditions took a decidedly intellectual bent, and the more people "talked" about the holy, the more they could understand it and the more "spiritual" they were—they thought.

> "Life without liberty is like a body without spirit."
> —Kahlil Gibran,
> essayist and poet

But a shift is happening when it comes to expanding our understanding of spirituality. We do not *have* bodies; we *are* bodies. Do you see the difference between these two ideas? Our spirits don't just reside in these physical vessels called a body; our very nerve synapses that create thought and the sinews that move us around *are* the stuff of spirit and soul. Spiritual experience, as part of human experience, is not separate from bodily perception. That wind on my face as I ski down the mountain is not just my body moving through air. It is also the very

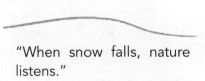

"When snow falls, nature listens."
—Antoinette van Kleeff,
Digital Scrapbooking Layout

experience of my place in the world. I get a deeper sense that *I am here in this world. I belong here. I have a place here on this earth.* And that sensation of wind on my face is also the physical manifestation of sensing the presence of something bigger than myself—*I am here and I am not alone.* I am part of, and moving through, creation itself. Amazing creation.

We were created to be able to sense the Creator, the creation, and our relationship to all of it. And we don't always need words for it to be real. Just sensing it in our bodies is enough for it to truly "be."

Just the other day I took a snowshoe hike. It had been snowing here in the Lake Tahoe area for a couple of weeks. Big and really light flakes had fallen steadily so that now a few feet had the ground covered with what looked like the fluffiest marshmallow creme you've ever seen. So my friends and I and their snow-loving dogs (actually, I haven't seen many dogs who don't love snow!) headed out to the end of my road to the stretch of forest there. The scene unfolded like this:

All my senses begin to pop. The slight wind perks up my ears to my all-time favorite sound—the wind moving among the tops of the giant pines. This sound never fails to slow me down to listen to it, and the hair on the back of my neck stands up as if reaching to feel the sway of the treetops. The other sound I hear is also one of the reasons I love winter—the sound of silence. The blanketed earth is muted so that even the sound of snowshoes on the trail is just a muffled crunch.

My vision fills with the artwork of winter. Every dark limb and boulder is covered with white frosting, and the dark/light contrast creates a gallery of achingly beautiful snapshots. I almost can't get anywhere on my trek because I keep stopping to behold each nature-made masterpiece. My retinas greedily drink it in. My eyes are drawn upward to the snow-capped steeples in this "church of the trees." They're drawn downward to the shapes, humps, and bumps of hidden obstacles in the path. I love the feel of snowshoes, their wide platform enabling me to step right on or over the obstacles in my path.

> "Joy is the feeling of grinning inside."
> —Melba Colgrove, *How to Survive the Loss of a Love*

Every once in a while a tree lets go, and I jump as a plop of snow drops. I feel the slap of snow on the back of my legs as the snowshoes kick it up behind me. My breathing is sometimes easy, sometimes labored with the ups and downs of the terrain. And my legs are going to love the hot bath I've promised them after this. Best of all, a taste of newly fallen snow, and the tickle on my tongue as it melts, give me a simple delight that I've needed in these hectic days.

On this particular afternoon, sight, sound, touch, and taste all combined to give me an experience of elation, an attitude of gratitude, and a connection to the heights and depths of my spirit. There's just no other way to get at these things besides through our actual physical body. The pupils of our eyes widen or narrow as they become the frames for the artwork of this world. The fragile hairs in our ears wiggle and ripple as waves of sound offer natural symphonies of the sacred. Even if we sit and meditate, our body is working to provide us with images that take us to the "nirvana" places we desire through the connection of synapses of memory and imagination. Our bodies are the stuff of spirit.

Reconnecting

The idea that our bodies are integral to our spirituality means that many, if not all, of us are dealing with obstacles to the depth of spirit we are meant to experience as humans. Each of us has inherited to some extent the ideas of body-mind-spirit split.

Many of us grew up with messages about our bodies being "bad" or "dirty" all by themselves without even considering what we *do* with or to our bodies. Some of us experienced situations where our bodies were not honored as sacred, and we live with the scars of abuse or oppression. Some of us were told not to show our emotions, disallowing some of the physical signs of deeply felt experience, such as crying or hugging. The history of the oppression of our bodies/spirits has taken a toll on our ability to celebrate the wonder of our physicality.

> "Why ski? Skiing through fresh powder snow and making your way down mile upon mile of mountain terrain is probably one of the greatest ways that you can find to experience freedom."
> —Warren Smith, *Go Ski: Read It, Watch It, Do It*

Being cut off from the sacred nature of our bodies as good and created miracles has caused a lot of pain, violence, and hatred in our world—and maybe in your life. But we can experience transformation through the activities of our bodies. Spiritual adventures in the snow—the thrill of achieving a great downhill run, the accomplishment of making an uphill on cross country trails, feeling the tension of life drain away as we hike along a snowy river, or even just filling our lungs with good, clean mountain air—can reconnect us with our bodies in ways that can be healing. Healing happens when we can let go of the old and destructive habits and messages that have been keeping body and spirit separated like an open wound. And this healing is essential for our spiritual growth.

Emotional healing can also begin when our bodies—where our emotions reside and through which they are expressed—get to experience freedom. Things that weigh us down can get "worked out" as our bodies engage in activities that bring release. Here's how it happened for Karen:

> Last winter was a snowboarding season like no other, and it left an indelible imprint on me. My sister lost her battle with cancer that November. When the snow started to fall in December, it took me by surprise. It was a sign that the world was going on as usual. I was both relieved and incensed. I moved through my days as if I weighed five hundred pounds and was slogging through mud. My familiar high-energy rhythm was but a distant memory. The only time my body felt like it could move with some normalcy was when I was on my board. Yet even then I could not escape the abyss of my grief. I was constantly reminded of the winter five years earlier when my sister was first diagnosed, while six months preg-nant. It was an excruciating time of waiting. Waiting for the baby to grow enough. Waiting to start treatment that desperately needed to begin. Waiting till the doctors thought it was time. Waiting for someone to tell us what was really real. Waiting to exhale. That winter, I spent countless hours on the back side ski lift in deep prayer, sending positive energy across three thousand miles to grow the baby, shrink the tumor. Shrink the tumor, grow the baby. Grow the baby, shrink the tumor.
>
> In the darker days of last winter, I sometimes despaired because it hadn't "worked," our prayers had

not been heard. But a good run on my snowboard would help me remember that it actually *had* worked. My nephew had almost five years to know and love his mom, and to thrive in her love. My customary joy continued to be elusive. But when I was on my board, carving through powder or catching some speed in the steeps, I could sense it hovering somewhere nearby, bringing me hope that it would indeed return some day.

For Karen, renewed hope was a physical experience. As she reconnected with her body through her movement on the slopes, life, healing, and insight awakened in her body amidst grief. The complexity of the body-mind-spirit connection offers many avenues for making these kinds of shifts from brokenness to wholeness. At times, thoughts and feelings may take the lead in transforming our states of being. In other instances, it will be the motion of our body that literally moves us over an abyss, hastening emotional and spiritual healing. Hope has a way of rising to the surface when we allow physical activity to move energy through our bodies, and when we connect with our passions.

> "Turn your wounds into wisdom."
>
> —Oprah Winfrey, television host

Spiritual Exercise

Beyond the healing of the body-mind-spirit split, there are also connections between exercise and spirituality. The term "spiritual exercise" may bring to mind something related to meditation, or praying, or thinking positive thoughts, or sitting and breathing deeply in a cross-legged pose. They're fine, but they're not exactly what I'm talking about here. Think about physical exercise: blood pumping faster, oxygen intake increased, muscles pushed to their limit, endurance stretched. Now consider that these things are a pathway to renewed vitality, opened perspective, new insights, and increased hope—all spiritual endeavors.

One of the most basic avenues to healing and reconnecting body, mind, and spirit is to breathe deeply. Many ancient peoples believed that spirit resided in their breath. Various spiritual traditions' stories of creation involve divine wind and breath blown into once inanimate beings to create life. Our vocabulary is rife with connotations deriving from this ancient belief. "Respiration," "inspiration," to "conspire," and "aspire" are all words from the Latin root *spirare*, meaning "to breathe." When someone is a "breath of fresh air," we consider them to be full of life and vigor. We now know that breath literally brings renewal to all of the body. Without a good supply of it, our life and spirit wane. Spiritual meditation practices consistently invite us to focus on our breath—the gentle rhythm of the intake and exhale—as a way of exercising our awareness and expanding our understanding of the connection to creation, to life, and to the Divine. When we literally and physically breathe more deeply, we open new possibilities for the airing out of things we've been holding in, tucked in the tight, hidden corners of our bodies.

> "It is exercise alone that supports the spirits, and keeps the mind in vigor."
> —Marcus Tullius Cicero, first-century Roman philosopher

After a particularly spectacular day of skiing in fresh "pow-pow" (you can't just call it "powder" when it is that good), I was fall-down-on-my-face wasted, exhausted, and quadriceps-trembling tired. The last run of the day had brought me to the end of a run that, thankfully, had Adirondack-style chairs sitting about ten feet away from the ski racks. It was all I could do to get the skis off, stumble over, and flop in an open seat. This was the kind of "tired" that was salve for my soul.

For months I had been burning the candle at both ends, working on great projects, but too many. I was juggling too many things and feeling the weight of too many deadlines. I was tired but wasn't sleeping well. I would lie awake thinking of all the expectations I couldn't possibly meet and would all of a sudden realize that I was breathing so shallowly that my chest was tight, and I was feeling lightheaded. I never thought I was the kind of person to have a panic attack, but I think I was mighty close. I was fall-on-my-face tired then, too, but it was a different kind of exhaustion. I was filling up with an anxiety-produced lactic acid in my body with no outlet.

So that day I skied until I couldn't anymore. And *that* kind of tired was the release valve for what was bottled up in me. After I pried myself out of the easy chair, I soaked in natural hot springs in a dimly lit sacred mountain cave revered by Native Americans for its healing minerals. I basked in the physical release of lactic acid from my screaming muscles, and the hot tears of release from stress; both were necessary to heal my soul. I have no doubt that nothing but the physicality of this experience could have brought such profound and swift relief.

"The endorphins are pumping through us wildly, like a snowmelt-fed creek, and our sense of well-being and utter happiness is sometimes just over-powering."
—John Lionberger, *Renewal in the Wilderness*

Just as physical symptoms, such as a tightened throat and chest or an upset stomach, can point to inner turmoil, so, too, can physical exertion lead to renewed spirit. Adrenaline, sweat, sore muscles—all the things we experience on the slopes—can contribute not only to our physical but also to our mental and spiritual health.

❄ A Reflective Moment

If you have come to the mountain for the first time and find yourself aching from your first day on the slopes, you can celebrate your spirit of adventure. You are doing something you've never done before, as evidenced by the hurting muscles you never knew you had. Celebrate your courage to experience something you may have never thought you could do. You are a spiritual adventurer!

Even if you have been skiing or riding since you were old enough to stand and you already define yourself as an adventurer, pushing yourself to new heights or landing that trick with the sun beaming down can still bring renewed passion that can carry over into the spirit of your everyday living—and that makes you a spiritual adventurer as well.

Whether a novice or veteran, what were you aware of in your body when you were out on the slopes? After you came in? What senses seemed to be strongest for you? Were you aware of holding anything in? Letting anything go? What got "connected" for you? How did you experience your body's activity as something that enlivened you spiritually?

Further, what can you do, and who can you be for good in the world, with that physical-spiritual high you have at the end of an exhilarating day on the mountain?

Psychologists have long been encouraging us to get out and exercise to keep depression and anxiety at bay. For many physical ailments, medical doctors are now telling us that physical exercise is as important as anything they prescribe. Consider this: You have just been given a different kind of prescription for what ails your soul. Go to the snow and have fun. Go find mountain air and breathe deeply. Go challenge yourself physically and see what happens to your spirit.

Conversation with an Adventurer
Alex Heyman, ski instructor

~

Alex Heyman is an avid skier, both in and out of bounds. He is the training coordinator for the Mountain Sports Learning Center at Sugar Bowl Ski Resort in North Tahoe. He is the author of a novel about spiritual epiphany in the wilderness titled *The Gift of Iguazu* and is working on a book on the mental aspects of skiing, including facing fear on the slopes. We talked with him about the issues he sees people facing during instruction and his love of the mountains.

When you are teaching people to ski or board, what helps people tune in more easily to the joy of skiing and boarding?
Skiing is an in-body experience. It is a very kinesthetic sport. People who tend to be more in their head usually have a harder time. They tend to get frustrated because they are struggling with thoughts of self-doubt. Sometimes a beginning-level skier can pick it up so quickly, and those are usually the ones that are in their body. They don't have to think about it too much. Kids catch on quicker because they don't yet have a lot of voices in their heads, and they are not as trained to process things in their heads before it gets down in the body.

How do you talk to adults about getting past their heads?
I will often start by saying, "Let's not focus on anything in particular right now. I just want you to notice what is going on in your body. Notice how your body is moving down the hill." It is about getting the focus in your body before you start to pick everything apart. And maybe also not getting too overly technical, because

you can get overloaded. Take one thing and incorporate it into your body awareness. I say, "Don't try to tell yourself what to do or tell yourself that you are not doing it well. Just put awareness in your body. Just notice." I use the term "soft focus": We are not concentrating hard; we are just noticing. There is a focus, but it's an awareness focus instead of trying to get it done at all costs.

How can we have the benefits of "soft focus" in our spiritual lives?

So many of us have voices going on ... whatever it is, doubt, judgment of self and others. Soft focus might be bringing your awareness to what you are doing. "Okay, that was me getting on myself." Or, "Oh, that was me judging that person." And then being careful not to judge myself for judging others—it can be a vicious cycle! When I've developed some practice in doing that, it has helped me be happier, for one thing, but also be able to interact with others and myself in a more peaceful way. And, to go back to the skiing, when I have a really present moment when I feel really alive, it is a very peaceful moment, I have peace. There is a direct relationship there. Skiing is a great metaphor for life.

What makes the difference for you between an ordinary ski day and a really amazing "in the Zone" day?

If I were to map out the most incredible day on skis, it would include powder. For me, skiing is connecting with the world around me, connecting with the mountains. I get to "dance around" with the mountains on the snow, and if I get to do it in two or three feet of deep powder with beautiful mountains all around, it's even better. And if I get to share it with some great friends, then that's where it is for me. And I guarantee you, I'm in my body when I'm there. I'm not getting down on myself for not doing it right. I'm just aware and really enjoying myself.

You talk about the awareness of the motion. What kind of "dance" with the mountain is your favorite kind of rhythm?

I change it up a lot. I can relate to speed. There is a lot of joy to be had in that. You have to be present when you are going fast or you might be in trouble. I really enjoy rhythm, too, especially in powder. We sometimes call it "the porpoise effect": when you make turns in the powder, you rise and sink to develop a rhythm. That is a phenomenal feeling for me. And combining that with speed is pretty nice, too! When I am in the backcountry, about 90 percent of the time is spent going uphill and only about 10 percent coming down. So it is more about being in the mountains and experiencing them—if you are open to it, connecting with that.

What about the risk factor in the backcountry? What kind of effect does that have?

Well, it definitely makes me ski more cautiously, I make more cautious decisions. A lot of mountaineers and backcountry skiers often do it for the risk factor, and it makes them feel alive, the adrenaline rush, the idea that I'm alive yet teetering on the edge of death. I can understand that, but I don't relate to it because I don't need to have that experience to feel alive. It is a matter of choice. People will go climb Everest or a similar mountain, spend thousands of dollars and all this time preparing for it, and maybe spend a couple of minutes at the top "feeling really alive," and I'm thinking, "What a huge amount of work to get to that point when you could do it right here, right now!" I'm convinced that it can happen in any environment, but it is much easier for me to feel really alive, really connected with a Source, when I'm in a wilderness environment. It feels like a "direct connection" for me.

Fear is such an incredible phenomenon in terms of how it resides in the mind, and it can paralyze you even in

places you wouldn't normally feel it, depending on your state of mind. How do you approach fear in your students?

I've been working on a book on the mental aspects of skiing, and fear is a big part of that. Fear resides in the mind but manifests in the body, and you can see it. Everything gets really tense. We want some tension, what you might call "functional tension"— actually firing our muscles and using them—but too much tension can be debilitating.

I don't have a set way that I help people with fear. It is a case-by-case basis. Sometimes it is just getting them to focus on something else. Other times, if they are really afraid and it's hampering their ability to do things, I'll just have them become aware of it. "I can tell that you are afraid right now. This time down, I want you to just notice what is happening in your body because of that." And they start to focus on their bodies, they become aware of the tension, and just being aware of it can release it sometimes. The mind affects the body, and the body affects the mind. If you have a big smile on your face, it is harder to be upset. If you get your awareness on where the tension is, you start to release that tension. Sometimes we just don't know the tension we are holding. I try to get them a little bit more comfortable until, a while later, they are laughing at the fear they had before. It is great practice for life. It would be great if more people could become just more aware. Skiing can be a great teacher for that.

3 I Could Kiss the Mountain

Getting Stoked on a Natural High

THOUGHTS FROM KAREN

Have you ever had the experience of being so blown away by beauty in the great outdoors that you wanted to laugh and cry at the same time? Or you wanted to applaud? Or pump your fist and shout YES? And your next thought was, "How in the world did it take me a lifetime to get here?" or "Why don't I do this more often?"

What is it about purple mountain majesties that lend themselves to profound spiritual experiences? And what happens in us to facilitate these soul-filling moments? The inexplicable wonders of snow and the breathtaking beauty of austere mountain vistas create the perfect environment for leaving the stresses of life behind in order to forge inspired connections with the natural world.

Stalking the Natural High

Come along with me for a moment on a few spiritual adventures of full immersion in the natural world. I hope they bring to mind some of your own mountain experiences and the subtle qualities that transform the ordinary into the extraordinary.

I finally make my way to the top of the ridgeline, having climbed for a long while. The last strides have been the steepest. My lungs are exploding, begging for more oxygen that is not there. The view opens before me, and my eyes drink it in, scarcely able to believe the beauty. How can someone look at such an awe-inspiring expanse and wonder whether there is some greater Intelligence at work? Pausing above the tree line, I seem to be literally on top of the world. The sun dances on the sloping milky surface below, creating a billion twinkling snow stars. Mountain vista after mountain vista unfolds in the distance where blue sky meets white craggy peak. What is it about mountains that fills my soul? I am flooded with a sense of overwhelming gratitude at the opportunity to stand on this spot. The effort of the climb cannot compare to the magnitude of this moment. Longtime local adventurers can gaze into the distance and name the peaks and passes as if they were all old friends, known for their particular quirks and personalities. They can recall a harrowing hike up one precipice, estimate with great confidence the altitude and snowpack of the next, and tell you the history of who perished on the adjacent pass in the 1800s. I vow to somehow, someday, know such intimacy with this unbelievable expanse, this body of God.

"My profession is always to be alert, to find God in nature, to know God's lurking places, to attend all the oratorios and the operas in nature."
—Henry David Thoreau, essayist, poet, and philosopher

Now join me deep in the woods on a delightfully snowy day (on any kind of sticks or shoes). I find myself entranced with the falling snowflakes. I watch and am fascinated as each slowly twists and turns, making its way to its resting place among a jillion others. I remember hearing that no two snowflakes are alike. Can this be possible? I look up and choose one to follow all the way to the ground. And then another. And another. And another. It is hypnotic, meditative. I simply cannot resist the childlike urge to close my eyes, tilt my head back with open mouth to catch, to taste these tiny miracles. It is an intensely sensory experience. Surely the Eskimo, with their multiple words for snow, have a word for "snow caught on tongue." Who in the world could ever have thought to create snow, this deliciously frozen water falling gently from the sky? I smile with appreciation and humility to the Great Imagination. I am filled with a sense of wonder. Overcome, I listen very carefully. Silence. Thunderous silence. The dramatic silence of snowfall is mesmerizing. I am completely engulfed. It would not be difficult to convince me that I have been transported to a different planet, so far removed do I feel. I whisper a prayer of thanksgiving for solitude, for silence, for snow.

No creature has ever loved snow more than my dog, Jasmine. She has no doubt that it all arrived just for her. In fact, she probably believes she conjured it up herself. She sticks her head down deep in the white fluff and takes a few breaths. Then she comes up giddily gasping and snorting and proceeds to throw the snow she dug with her nose up over her back. Jaz then prances around in circles a few times, plops down, and rolls in it while biting playfully at the flakes. She gets up and shakes, looks at me with a delighted look on her face, then proceeds to do it all again. She has been known to mischievously try to push me down into the snow and to slide down a small hill on her back. I marvel at her ability to relish each present moment, this spiritual teacher of rollicking joy and unconditional love.

"To be aware of little quiet things, however, you need to be quiet inside. A high degree of alertness is required. Be still. Look. Listen. Be present."

—Eckhart Tolle, *A New Earth: Awakening to Your Life's Purpose*

The next adventure begins as I round the precipice, and my breath is taken away by the scene that explodes in my sight, that crown jewel of the Sierra Nevada, the majestic Lake Tahoe. I marvel at this lake created millions of years ago by faults—formations of land rising and sinking. I can see the Carson Range formed by a fault on the east side of the lake. The Sierra Nevada rise out of the waters on the western margin. The transporting of some of the earth's crusty layer constructed the mountain pinnacles of the Tahoe area, along with Lake Tahoe itself. The lake's basin is composed of granite, creating an effective filter against sediment, allowing the water to remain astoundingly clear. This magnificent lake is so deep it never freezes, even in Tahoe's frigid temperatures. I point downhill, convinced that I will end up with a splash right into the lake, so close does it appear. Dazed at Mother Nature's brilliance through the ages, I am filled with gratitude, aware that many in the world never get to lay eyes on such beauty.

> "The only sound I hear is my own breathing, the 'poosh' sound of my ski poles punching holes in the snow, and the hiss of my skis. This is truly sublime, and I am feeling very content, very peaceful."
>
> —John Lionberger, *Renewal in the Wilderness*

Now I embark at dusk on a snowshoe hike into high mountain meadows. When I reach the trees, it is like entering a black-and-white photograph. All colors have faded to shades of gray, and the stark contrast of bright snow and shadowy trees sharpens my vision. I have hiked in near darkness, allowing the silence of the woods to overtake me. The darkness forces me into anonymity, hiding me until I'm nearly invisible. I glance regularly at the ridgetops for hints of my anticipated heavenly companion. Finally, she announces herself with a faint glow, revealing the peak. I stop and watch until her upper arc just clears the mountaintop. I am awed by her presence. Already, at a fraction of her total, she makes long shadows with my body. Somehow, both gradually and quickly, she rises up over the mountain and presents herself— large, radiant, yellow-mottled orb, turning the sky from black to deep midnight blue. I gasp at her grandeur. It is as if someone has turned on a light. Meadows seem as bright as the noonday sun, and dark woods are fully illuminated. I continue my hike mesmerized, my gaze never leaving "my" spectacular moon for more than a few seconds. It was a dramatic experience of being found.

Finally, follow me as I slowly traverse the terrain on my chariot—the modern-day chair lift. I marvel at the statuesque trees. They are heavily laden with snow, branches bending down with too much weight, pointing proudly to the snow around their trunks even as it piles up to engulf them. When I emerge from the lift and head down a run, I am startled to see a lone coyote standing square in the middle of the trail just a few yards ahead. I slow to a stop just as it turns its head to look me over. The two of us are the only creatures in sight. We study each other for what seems like an intense long moment. Are we playing chicken or "stare-down"?

"Wild beasts and birds are by right not the property merely of people who are alive today, but the property of unknown generations whose belongings we have no right to squander."
—Theodore Roosevelt, twenty-sixth president of the United States

I dare not flinch. I want to remember this moment, this privilege of sharing space with this wily but majestic creature. I am struck with a powerful revelation that this is his (or her) space, not mine. I am the visitor, the one out of place, the one encroaching and invading. Indigenous and native peoples have long espoused the philosophy that the land does not belong to us, but we belong to the land. A ridiculous idea, if you ask our culture of greed. We would do well to reconsider. Just ask the coyote.

What Shifts?

Author and public speaker David J. Wolpe relates a wonderful Hasidic story in *Teaching Your Children about God* about the child of a rabbi who used to wander in the woods. At first the father let the child wander, but over time he became concerned. The woods were dangerous. The father did not know what lurked there. He decided to discuss the matter with his child. One day he took the child aside and said, "You know, I have noticed that each day you walk into the woods. I wonder, why do you go there?

The child said, "I go there to find God."

"That is a very good thing," the father replied gently. "I am glad you are searching for God. But don't you know that God is the same everywhere?"

"Yes," the child answered, "but I'm not."

This story speaks volumes about what we experience when we remove ourselves from the usual hectic pace of our lives and go do something different, be somewhere different. Adventures in the snow afford us this opportunity, whether we are skiing, riding, snowshoeing, or whatever passion we choose. When we can let go, even for a while, of the demands to increase the speed of our lives, to multitask, to hurry, hurry, hurry so that we can do more, buy more, and be more, a shift can occur. The shift brings such relief that it feels like a lifeline; we know who we are once again. The opportunity to reconnect with ourselves and with the Creator and creation in places of awe-inspiring beauty may be one of the greatest gifts we can give ourselves and, if done often enough, may well change the course of our lives.

> "You are never more essentially, more deeply, yourself than when you are still."
> —Eckhart Tolle, *A New Earth: Awakening to Your Life's Purpose*

As the father shared with his child, it is perhaps true that God is the same everywhere, but we are surely not. Exactly how is it that we are different on the mountain, and why? What is the source of this transformational opportunity? What shifts almost imperceptibly until we realize we are different?

Consider your own soul-filling moments in your favorite outdoor cathedral. What happens may seem to take you out of yourself, but it actually plunges you more deeply into yourself. This is where a hunger and an opening converge. A sense of wonder and mystery rises up, and you may marvel that you are an insignificant speck among the grandeur and, clearly, you are not in charge. (What a relief!) In part, it is the quality of being fully present that makes it a spiritual moment.

Being fully present means to be fully aware. It means finding a degree of stillness in our bodies and our minds. It means not being consumed with today's project deadlines, what we are making for dinner, picking up the kids, paying bills, our doctor's appointment, calling our mom—all of the mind clutter that usually takes up space in our consciousness. Instead, we are aware of our breathing, of our sensory perceptions. We are acutely tuned-in to what is taking place around us in the immediate moment.

It is amazing how much we are capable of missing when we are not fully present. We can blast down a mountain slope intent on reaching our destination—lunch or the next lift—and never even become conscious of the beauty of the snow, the majestic mountains in the distance, the laughter of kids. But being fully present can take an ordinary experience and make it extraordinary. Sometimes we are able to become fully present when we have an ebullient sensory experience that creates an intimate connection between us and something larger. We drink in the beauty with our eyes, surveying and honoring every detail. We savor each sound as it reaches our ears—birdsong and wind rustle. We inhale and relish the fragrance of pine resin mingled with the cool pristine mountain air. We become conscious of the soft breeze caressing our skin, and it becomes a gentle kiss from the Divine. We receive it as we would an extravagant gift.

I am compelled to add here that, while I understand the impulse to ride or ski with an earbud connected to an iPod, jamming to your favorite tunes, I invite you instead (at least some of the time) to savor and relish the sounds of yourself ripping through snow, squirrels chirping, shouts of jubilance. The "woo-hoo" you miss may be your own!

These sensory experiences may arrive in your awareness sequentially or concurrently, but the longer you are able to fully immerse yourself in the experience, the more the subtle, incremental details will reveal themselves. At first you may notice a wisp of a cloud lazily unfurling itself just above a distant mountain peak, the distinctive reddish tinge of ponderosa pine bark. Then, you may become aware of the slowing of your pulse as you sink into a more relaxed but attentive state. It is at this point that the boundaries of where you begin and end start to fade. The experience becomes more visceral and your (self-imposed) isolation falls away. This is the beginning of feeling at one with all creation. There is no longer "you" and everything else. There is only one integrated whole of which you are a part; your separateness is but an illusion.

Award-winning poet and author Kathleen Norris was perhaps the first to coin the term "spiritual geography" to describe how it is that we become so affected by dirt, hills, plants, valleys, seasons, rocks, snow, trees, and weather that our inner landscapes somehow merge with the outer world. In discussing her writing of *Dakota: A Spiritual Geography*, she says, "At its Greek root, geography means 'writing about a place,' and the vast, almost sculptured landscape of the western Dakotas has a spiritual quality that I couldn't ignore. 'Spiritual geography' also describes the way a place shapes people's attitudes, beliefs, myths. The spiritual geography of the plains is complex. But the stark beauty of the land—its strength—also inspires strength in people."

> "All of us are born mystics, for the capacity to experience wonder and a primal sense of connectedness with all life is our birthright."
> —Ann Gordon, writer

The spiritual geography of the mountains moves me like nowhere else. It feels as if these mountains live in my soul. When I am away from them, I feel off balance and disoriented. I return home and inexplicably feel my equilibrium return, and I feel myself breathing deeply and more slowly again in the crystal clear mountain air. If the plains inspire strength in people, the mountains surely inspire the awareness to slow down and experience our own sense of wonder.

So what is it that happens in us when we do that? Nothing changes—and yet everything changes. We see with new eyes, hear with new ears, and breathe as if for the first time. We drink in beauty with our whole beings. We feel a profound connection to the natural world and know at a primal level that we are both a part of it, and one with it.

The Awe Experience

Although the young child in the rabbi's story likely would not have expressed it like this, another contributing factor to the child's altered state in the natural world was his/her capacity to experience awe. The spiritual adventures described at the opening of this chapter were, for me, adventures that scored high on the "awe meter." I like the way Rabbi Jamie Korngold (see the "Conversation with an Adventurer" at the end of chapter 4) defines awe in her book *God in the Wilderness*: "the ineffable emotion we experience when we step outside the realm of humanity and realize the mystery of the universe."

Rabbi Korngold suggests that one of the obstacles to experiencing awe is the culture we find ourselves living in. I think she's right on target: we're "over-awed" by "our jet-set, Internet era of scientific discovery, technological advancement, extreme sports, and adventure collecting." We, too, often get to the place where we don't even notice the awesome; our sense of awe has been dulled. As Rabbi Korngold points out, when "our knowledge and control of nature increases, the mystery of the world decreases." To remedy this dire situation, I join her call to "recalibrate our awe-meters."

Children are experts on awe. They can experience snow, mud, the moon, the stars—whatever catches their attention—as if every time were the first time. Even months after my family gushed over the first hummingbirds of the season, my son Zachary, who was four at the time, still dramatically shushed everyone and pointed with great reverence and appreciation each time they returned to the feeder. Awe. Childlike awe. A spiritual practice worth indulging to help us find our true selves and our true connections once again.

Perhaps even more transformative, these spiritual adventures in the snow can somehow enable us to take off our serious, responsibility-laden, "adult" personas and reclaim our childlike jump-up-and-down, run-around-in-circles selves, free to feel awe and joy in our bodies with reckless abandon.

> "Perhaps the spiritual richness is precipitated by the stark beauty of the wilderness ... by that feeling of smallness within the largeness. We wonder at the mystery of creation, we marvel at the Creator. Or perhaps it is all of these elements building upon one another, generating a veritable cascade of spiritual opportunity."
> —Rabbi Jamie Korngold,
> *God in the Wilderness*

Ski instructor, backcountry skier, and spiritual seeker Alex Heyman (see the "Conversation with an Adventurer" at the end of chapter 2), acknowledging how difficult it is to put into words, explains, "Being in the mountains, I may be hiking the Tahoe Rim trail, for example, and I see a stunning-looking mountain. I just stare at it for a while, just take it in. And there is a huge ... you can describe it how you want ... but a huge transfer of energy, if you are open to it. It is this amazing experience."

I resonate with the transfer of energy Alex describes. I would take it a step further and suggest that we are not separate, static entities, but that dynamically connected sources of energy flow between us. We can shut our eyes (and hearts) to that possibility and never experience it, or we can engage in it and be blown away by its power to change us. As we recognize the deep hunger of our souls for such experiences, we will likely feel drawn to more and more such spiritual adventures.

Wordless Bliss

The little child in the woods was also on to something else. Though one so young may not have had words to explain why going into the woods to find God was important, this child somehow knew that getting "away" was the key to accessing the gifts of solitude. When we find ourselves in the absence of others from the human species, we are able to explore the inner contours of our beings at a depth we could never hope to reach in the presence of others. I have had many experiences snowboarding where I have realized, in the middle of a run, that I am the only person I can see. Often in these moments, I have stopped to relish this realization, to sigh, to be fully present to it, and to drink it in. I have actively sought out such opportunities for solitude in cross country skiing and snowshoe hiking. In the noisy hurry-up world in which we live, there is no substitute for finding ourselves enraptured in the restorative beauty of nature, captivated by silent, soul-filling aloneness.

At some point in the experience of solitude, our analyzing brain is invited to take a break, and our creative, intuitive brain is invited to play a more active role. We can let go of that part of ourselves that is our list maker, planner, organizer of details, the judge of all things, and we can access the part that recognizes our connection to the universe. With what has been called our "left" brain quiet of its usual mind chatter—arguing with a relative, worrying about some future

> "Language ... has created the word 'loneliness' to express the pain of being alone. And it has created the word 'solitude' to express the glory of being alone."
> —Paul Johannes Tillich, theologian and philosopher

event, making "to-do" lists—our so-called "right" brain can engage. It can transport us to the blissful state of being completely immersed in beautiful surroundings, fully in tune with the amazing aliveness of our bodies, exulting in the experience of being immersed in snow.

Words fall away and become completely unnecessary, even irrelevant. In fact, words can often get in the way of spiritual experiences. In the solitude of a mountain vista or deep in the woods, we can honor the gift we are receiving by experiencing it without words. Though we may be much more comfortable with conversation and company, there are immense rewards in seeking out times of reflective silence. In this greater expanse of connection, we may find ourselves enveloped in the Mystery of it all. Fully transcendent. Such experiences are often accompanied by sighs of contentment, whoops of delight, shouts of "YES!" We may be overcome by the urge to break into song, even (and especially) if we don't think of ourselves as singers. We become awestruck participants in this profound moment in time. And we know we will never be the same.

❋ A *Reflective Moment*

Take a few moments to remember and meditate on some snowy spiritual geographies that have impacted you. Where were they? On mountaintops in a snowstorm? Beside frozen lakes? In the woods? Next to snow-lined rivers? Go there in spirit. Linger there. Have the experience again for yourself. What was it about the location, the beauty, the sounds and smells that made it so special? What was it that made you different? What made it unforgettable?

Resolve to take yourself to places where the spiritual geography merges with your inner landscapes, places that you do not merely visit but that become a part of you.

Conversation with an Adventurer

Bill Seline, backcountry skier, mountain guide, and telemark ski instructor

~

Bill Seline is a certified avalanche instructor and also a paramedic and captain of his local fire department. If you can't find Bill, he may be skiing in the backcountry for several days at a time. He has skied the backcountry of the Tetons, Rockies, Cascades, and Sierras, as well as Alaska, France, and Switzerland.

How did you get into backcountry skiing?

I skied for about sixteen years from age two to eighteen, then I took up telemark skiing because I was a little bored with downhill skiing. Taking up teleskiing was really rewarding. Learning something new was challenging in itself. Once I had some telemark skills, I started going out into the backcountry. I thought that backcountry skiing would be about making different turns down the slope, but it was more serendipitous. The first thing I noticed was the peace I felt. I quickly realized that I could slap on the skins and take off and quickly be away from it all. In the backcountry I found I could think clearly and could often come up with some of my best ideas or solutions to problems. It is a very mind-clearing activity for me.

How do you prepare for immersing yourself in the wilderness of the backcountry?

There are inherent risks in backcountry skiing, so there is much to plan for, like avalanche safety, navigation skills and route plans so I don't get lost, first aid, and self- and team-rescue skills. An injured knee in the backcountry is a much bigger deal than at the ski area, as you can imagine. These risks add to the excitement about being "out there." The feeling and experiences are much more intense when I know there are bigger consequences. Keeping myself from being caught in an avalanche, for instance, requires lots of attention to nature—how did the snow fall here, what were the winds like, what is the underlying slope configuration, is this slope steep enough to cause avalanches that could get me? So as I travel through the mountains, I often feel that I am not only witnessing nature but going a step further, visualizing the process of nature in regard to the snow, for example.

I was skiing a few weeks ago with my wife, Wendy, on the backside of Mt. Judah. We were looking for some sweet corn on the southeast face. Skiing the upper section, we were aware that it had been very warm, and the snow was losing stability fast. As we carefully made our way down the slope, Wendy kicked off a wet slide that started moving slow and then picked up speed. Luckily, we were anticipating that, and we quickly skied out of the slide path to lower-angle terrain. Once we were safe, we talked about how we try to understand what's going on in nature, but there are so many variables that it's hard to be right 100 percent of the time. We were feeling very aware and very alive as we thought about the potential consequences.

In backcountry skiing, what is the "climb" about for you?

The "climb" is spiritual for me. I continually get the confirmation that there is something big controlling things. It's like thinking about the symphony or the complexities of the human body and realizing that there is something much bigger that has a hand in things. I feel this way when I watch nature at work on my climb up. I find myself in constant awareness and wonderment. Travel in the backcountry is relatively slow as I move up the mountain with climbing skins on my skis. Some people may think of this slow climb as a waste of time with the advent of high-speed lifts, but I see it as an opportunity to immerse myself in the beauty of the mountains. On Donner Peak, I am always amazed at the wind-shaped juniper trees and how many years of frequent wind from the southwest that it took to shape a growing tree. The other day I noticed a beautiful woodpecker sitting on a branch of one of those trees—looking like he was contemplating where to start drilling. The weather is always new—the shapes of the clouds and the colors at sunrise or sunset fill my heart with energy. Every time I go out, even if it is to the same spot, there are things that are different; it is always a reminder that there are bigger powers at work, and I am just witnessing.

Stopping every few turns to admire your perfectly laid tracks is part of backcountry skiing for many. The sense of accomplishment is big, too: completing a tour or peak; climbing early in the morning; working through the personal pain one step at a time; dealing with the mountaineering challenges, risk, weather, maybe less-than-ideal skiing conditions; maybe doing something that you are not sure you can do; reaching the top, tearing the skins off, having a sip of tea, taking in the view, talking about the beauty with your buddy, then dropping down the run and making it safely back to the car. The drive back home is emotional for me; I feel ready to take on anything. Sometimes the more difficult it is, the more rewarding it is.

How is it that you are different when you are out in the natural world and how does this impact your experience?

Being in the backcountry reminds me that nature is in charge. In everyday life I often feel like I'm in the driver's seat and that I can fix anything with an e-mail, a phone call, money, or whatever. But on the mountain, nature is in charge. I was skiing in the Alps last spring, in the Bernese Oberland in Switzerland. The weather was beautiful as we skied for a few days around crevasse-covered glaciers, climbed peaks, and skied long powder runs. One day, feeling like we were in charge, we had clouds blow in in the middle of a beautiful day. Now we were using all of our map, compass, and GPS navigation skills on the largest glaciers in the Alps trying to find our way back to the hut. Winding our way between crevasses the entire afternoon, we were nail-biting scared, hoping we wouldn't fall into a crevasse and that we could find the needle in the haystack of white! I thought about it over dinner that night in the cozy hut. Many ski mountaineers die in the backcountry, and I couldn't help but think that many of them thought they could outdo or "manage" nature. Every year I get reminded that we are not in charge. This probably makes it more exciting—feeling the power of nature. I enjoy giving it the respect it deserves.

4 Freezing Your Fanny Can Be Spiritual?

Opportunities of the Winter Season

THOUGHTS FROM KAREN

W HAT IS IT ABOUT THE SEASON of winter that makes it an ideal time for spiritual reflection? This stark, barren time of year is rich with metaphor, as well as harsh reality in some climates, making it ideal for exploring our innate, albeit universal, cycles of life. It is a season full of dichotomies and contrasts. As aptly expressed by literature professors and authors Gary Schmidt and Susan M. Felch in *Winter: A Spiritual Biography of the Season* (SkyLight Paths), "Winter is that time of a frozen spirit, or even a desolate spirit, a time when activity and life and love slow and then still; it is the winter of our discontent, and its temperature is invoked in ways generally unpleasant: 'cold shoulder,' 'cold-blooded,' 'cold steel,' 'cold comfort.'... But it is also sliding down the hill ... laughing with the snow in your face, and running in to the fireplace, where the cider is heating well and maple logs are sending their sweet smoke up the chimney."

The unique characteristics of the winter season make it the perfect time for spiritual pondering and renewal. Our ancestors of ancient times feared that when the sun retreated behind the horizon, it might not reappear. So they performed ceremonies to coax it to return. Determined to retain some light for themselves, they placed fire at the focal point of the ceremonies. These ancient ones believed that if fire were continuously safeguarded, it would be a constant reminder of the sun. At times when the sun did reemerge, these communities engaged in festivities to mark the occasion. Sometimes they deemed it important to give offerings to the god or goddess they believed created the light, to influence its coming back.

Spiritual meaning has a way of perpetuating itself over time, from ancient rituals to modern. Our own winter celebrations and traditions carry traces of these ancient observances. The simplest practices of lighting candles on cold winter evenings, making home cozy and intimate with fire in the fireplace, provide a sense of assurance and expectancy that has been passed down through the ages. Even more so, our lighting of Hanukkah menorahs, Advent wreaths, and Kwanzaa candles embodies in family and community the quest for meaning and encouragement found in these ancient rituals.

> "Winter is the time of promise because there is so little to do—or because you can now and then permit yourself the luxury of thinking so."
>
> —Stanley Crawford,
> *Travel Notes*

Winter has long been thought of as a time of uncertainty, of fear, of loss and sorrow. The death of plants, the hibernation of animals, the freezing over of waterways, the barrenness of trees and landscapes mimic our own deaths, inviting us to face our mortality. We become aware that our lives are indeed uncertain, and we are beckoned to hold them precious, to live with intention.

Not so unlike the ancient fire builders, our longing for light urges us to search for the faith and hope that assures us that spring will come again. This primal opportunity opens spiritual places within, ripe for reflection, for pondering mystery, for connecting in intimate ways with the cycle of the seasons. It can be a time of putting into practice the wise example taught by the earth of relinquishing, letting go, and allowing parts of ourselves to lie fallow for a time.

What is in us that we might be better off without? What patterns of behavior, what long-held beliefs about ourselves or others, what attitudes or assumptions need to be discarded? What holds us back, weighs us down, and inhibits our ability to thrive? What needs to die in us so that new growth, new opportunity can burst forth?

Embracing Darkness

When we observe the history of human society, we can trace a long legacy of fear, discomfort, and even hatred of darkness and all things dark. Centuries of religious dogma have steeped us in the idea that "darkness is evil," and our culture continues to inundate us with images of "darkness as evil" by dressing villains in black, or at least darker than the other characters, in everything from *The Lion King* to *Star Wars*.

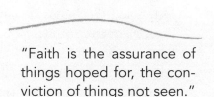

We are conditioned to think of darkness as something to be feared and dreaded, and it is not hard to see how this has fanned the flames of racism. I have often told the story of a little girl who sits in church and hears fervent admonition after admonition to "move away from the darkness, come out of the darkness, hate the darkness, and come into the light, love the light" and "the darkness is bad, and only the light is good." She looks down at her skin and is horrified to see that it is dark. What does this do to her psyche? What is the effect on her spiritual well-being?

"Faith is the assurance of things hoped for, the conviction of things not seen."
—Hebrews 11:1

We need a soulful attitude adjustment. We need to embrace the darkness of the natural world as the wonderful and miraculous gift that it is. After all, what would our lives be like if the sun (while a necessary and life-giving resource for which we are grateful) shone twenty-four hours each day? Many Alaskans who experience this situation for a short time each summer know that too

"There is a privacy about it which no other season gives you.... In spring, summer and fall people sort of have an open season on each other; only in winter, in the country, can you have longer quiet stretches when you can savor belonging to yourself."

—Ruth Stout, pioneer organic gardener and writer

much of a good thing has its own difficulties. The darkness is also a phenomenal gift—a protective covering under which to be with ourselves, to find a much slower pace, to relish gaps of quietude and contentment. Out of this rhythm, we can source the healing and renewal that can come only from releasing ourselves to the opportunity of living with less light.

Nature herself is our model for embracing the darkness. It is in the dark that embryos are nurtured and miraculously grow into babies. It is in the darkness of the soil that seeds germinate and ready themselves, finally bursting open to send their probing shoots up through the earth. In the dark of forests in dens, burrows, and nests, animals lie dormant, hibernating through the winter.

The longer nights and shorter days with their colder temperatures (in most climates), although depressing for some, gift us with a time for hunkering in, spending more hours sleeping or in restful states, replenishing after extended periods of heightened activity. This is true for our souls as well as our bodies. We may find we long to spend more time reading curled up by the fire, consuming hot meals of comfort, enjoying quality family time playing games or working puzzles.

Winter nighttime, which begins in the late afternoon in many geographies, offers us an ideal opportunity for literally embracing the dark. The only requirements, depending on your climate, are warm clothing and a sense of adventure. Become playmates with the night by going on a night hike with flashlights (in a familiar area for safety, of course). At various times throughout the hike, turn off the flashlights and experience the darkness through your senses. Notice how your eyes adjust and what they can see. Listen to the sounds of the night. What can you smell? Explore the contours of a nearby tree with your fingertips. Wonderful chances for making memories and enjoying bonding experiences among family and friends abound.

Take some time to learn about the stages of the moon and the moon's orbit during each month. Especially while in the mountains away from "light pollution" of major cities, learn and identify constellations. Spend a while marveling at the night sky and all that is revealed the more you gaze. Consider that the patterns and copious nature of the stars have been likened to the billions of synapses in our brains. Ponder this mirror effect and know that you really are one with this amazing universe. Opportunities to explore the gifts of darkness are as accessible as the light switch to your outstretched hand.

> "Everything has its wonders, even darkness and silence, and I learn whatever state I am in, therein to be content."
> —Helen Keller, deaf-blind author and political activist

Have you ever had the experience of having the power go off and getting settled in with a fire and candles, being so cozy and warm in the delicious quiet, reveling in the challenge, only to be disappointed by the jolt of overstimulation when the power comes back on? Then you laugh at yourself, remembering that you are the one who turns on the switches, that you do have choices. Some families make it a spiritual practice to live without electricity for one night a week for just these reasons. Care to be adventurous and try it?

With the invention of electricity and all of its ensuing "advances," particularly our modern age of entertainment and technology, we have lost touch with these natural rhythms intended for our lives and our bodies. We have only to look just outside our own neighborhoods on an autumn day to find animals gathering food for the winter or shoring up their winter homes in

"I prefer winter and fall, when you feel the bone structure of the landscape— the loneliness of it, the dead feeling of winter. Something waits beneath it, the whole story doesn't show."

—Andrew Wyeth, realist painter

preparation for a long winter's rest. Trees and plants shed their leaves for more efficient use of energy in a time of dormancy. Perhaps if we allow ourselves— even just a bit—to relish as gifts these opportunities of the winter, we might find ourselves mysteriously more connected and in tune with the natural rhythms of our earth and the wonders that await us beyond our front door. In doing so, we might be surprised to discover that we also feel more spiritually alive and more connected with the deepest parts of ourselves.

Feeling Alive

You may be thinking that exciting snow adventures are the antithesis to the kind of winter revival I am describing. To the contrary, both methods of savoring the opportunities of the winter season can be fully integrated, yielding fruitful results of spiritual awakening. Even while adventuring in the snow, whether blasting through thigh-deep powder or engaging in a leg-burning snow-shoe or skate-skiing workout, you may find your awareness heightened to marvel at the snow-laden tree limbs. You may find your sense of wonder reaching childlike proportions as you stop for a moment to take in the miracle of zillions of tiny white flecks floating carelessly in freefall. You may be awestruck by the intricacy of your own body, lithe and agile as it torques and contracts, gliding over snowy terrain. These moment-by-moment journeys may well transport you to an amplified sense of connectedness with yourself, with the universe, and with the One With All That Is.

Even the cold can be a conduit for waking us out of our mechanistic sleepwalking through our days. When cold air reaches the nerve endings on my skin, it is as if they are standing up and shouting and thrilled to be alive. "I can feel! I am alive! I am here!" It is completely invigorating and sends energy through my cells and entire being. I want to let roar a primal growl of affirmation (and often do). I am acutely present to where frigid wind crosses the border of the warm home of my body. Just as the sun slowly warms a frozen landscape early in the morning and the solidified ground begins to crackle as it softens and comes back to life, so my body awakens to the cold with a renewed sense of connection to all things. For those of you who have a strong distaste for the cold, there is a saying, "There is no such thing as bad weather, only bad clothing." The same technology that keeps astronauts warm in space is available to keep us warm in the coldest of winters. Pile on those layers, and go enjoy!

> "In a way winter is the real spring, the time when the inner things happen, the resurge of nature."
> —Edna O'Brien, Irish novelist and short-story writer

Winter's brashness also makes her a ruthless headmistress. She can force her students to learn—usually the hard way—a healthy respect for weather that can change in the blink of an eye and a sense of reverence toward the unexpected. Such lessons are not easily forgotten.

Some years ago, two of my favorite ski buddies and I—three musketeers that included one skier, one blader (extremely short skies), and one boarder—were having a glorious day skiing at Whistler Blackcomb resort in Vancouver, British Columbia, Canada. We were high on one of the peaks, above the tree line, when seemingly out of nowhere a cloud descended on the mountain. What had been a sunny "bluebird day" was now (at least up on the peak) becoming grayer and darker by the minute. The wind was howling and became more and more fierce. It was the kind of wind that makes you want to duck down and cover your head. Before we knew it, we were in complete whiteout.

None of us had ever experienced anything like it. There was no depth perception whatsoever, meaning it was not possible to detect the contour of the earth beneath us or where it might fall away. The cloud was so thick we could scarcely see our gloves when we held them in front of our faces. The only way we knew which way was up and which was down was the physical sensation of gravity that connected us to our skis and board. We could not discern at all where the trail was, let alone the edges of the trail that led to drop-offs plunging hundreds of feet below. Doing our best to gather our wits about us, we began to point out to each other the small, intermittently visible, neon green and orange markers that were (thankfully) placed at intervals along the trail. We took turns with one of us going first, slowly inching our way down toward the only marker we could just make out. Determined to stay together, we waited until all three of us got there. Then another of us led the way to the next marker. And then the next one, and the next.

"In the depth of winter, I finally learned that within me there lay an invincible summer."
—Albert Camus, author and philosopher

We proceeded in this way for what seemed an eternity until we had descended enough that the whiteout had abated somewhat. Finally, we were able to distinguish navigable terrain. Although one musketeer experienced vertigo so severe she had to stop for the day, we celebrated a moment of relief and gratitude to be alive. A renewed and stronger bond grew among us out of sharing such a harrowing experience. It was an adventure that we retell with great enthusiasm to this day. And our awe of the unpredictable power of winter to render us vulnerable and insignificant in the blink of an eye will remain with us always.

This presents an intriguing paradox. What is it about a brush with death that can make us feel so very alive? (Okay, it may be a bit of a stretch to call this one a near-death experience, even if its peril does get exaggerated each time we tell it!) I think it's because we rise to the challenge that Mother Nature lays at our feet, literally, whether expected or unexpected, and the adrenaline surge of the effort, followed by the triumph over the challenge, has us celebrating life in a whole new way.

"Let It Snow, Let It Snow, Let It Snow"

No discussion of winter would be complete without paying homage to that amazing yet tiny entity that changes our world and our lives—the snowflake. It colors everything white and silences the earth, makes our days all at once more difficult and more playful. Nothing can conjure up childhood memories of raucous joy and full-body play quite like snow. Recalling the "schools closed" announcement on TV or radio can still make me want to dance and shout. Snow sneaks our "inner kid" out to play in spite of us. It can do us immense good to discard for a moment the "mature," more serious grown-up images we have of ourselves. Is it possible for any of us to stand in a world whose hard edges have been made soft and rounded, where white fluff is poised to catch us and cushion us from life's harsh realities, where we are overwhelmed by the magnitude of a world gone completely silent and *not* have our spirits awakened to awe and wonder?

What is it that draws so many of us to this amazing white frozen delicacy that falls from the sky to grace us as manna from heaven? Since the

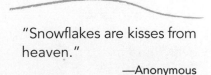

"Snowflakes are kisses from heaven."

—Anonymous

beginning of time, humanity has been drawn to water. Beyond water's necessary sustenance for the body, the human species has long found that deep yearnings have been quenched by the tranquility, beauty, and immensity of bodies of water. We need look only as far as the real estate listings of a coastal area, where properties designated "waterfront" or having a "view" are worth far more than their landlocked counterparts nearby. Perhaps this ingrained fascination with all things water is part of why so many of us find snow utterly irresistible.

All things are made new again with each snow. Everything gets another chance at a cleaner, quieter start. Like a bonus. Like getting to have a "do-over." Like life. Yes. YES! I think of every snowfall as a chance to begin again, to start over. Each individual snowflake is playing its part in silencing all that has been, creating an opening for something new.

Snowflakes are a prime example of nature's perfect synthesis of science and art. Snowflakes and snow crystals are, of course, formed from ice. Kenneth Libbrecht, Cal Tech physicist and snowflake expert extraordinaire, tells us that a snow crystal is a single crystal of ice. But a snowflake can be one snow crystal, several snow crystals bound together, or sizable clusters of crystals that create what Libbrecht terms "puffballs" that drift down from the clouds.

"Rounding every corner, smoothing every rough edge, quieting the din of our busy-ness, hushing (even if only for a moment) the crash of the world's brutality, covering every trash heap and dumpster, snow reminds us of the grace of God that makes everything brand new."

—Robert Lee Hill, author and minister

Snowflakes, however, are not simply raindrops that freeze. At times, drops of rain do become frozen as they fall; this is called sleet. But sleet cannot compete with the ornate, intricate patterns revealed in snow crystals. Libbrecht's devoted study of these mysterious entities reveals that the simplest shape of a snow crystal is a hexagonal prism. Technically, a hexagonal prism contains two faces that are hexagonal and six faces that are rectangular, but for those of us who are geometrically chal-

lenged, think of two parallel stop signs, and connect them, forming six additional sides.

Snow crystals are mostly in these hexagonal prism shapes
when they are tiny. As they grow, "arms" or "branches" spread
out, forming more complicated
shapes. Libbrecht goes on to
explain that even as the crystal
grows, it is blown around within
the cloud. As it encounters dif-
fering temperature pockets, the
six arms of the snow crystal
change and expand. Since all six
arms seek similar moisture and
temperature levels concurrently,
they all grow in similar ways,
creating a nearly symmetrical,
intricate structure of six branches. However, because the flakes
and crystals travel their own individual paths through the
clouds, each one looks a little different.

> "How full of the creative
> genius is the air in which
> these are generated! I
> should hardly admire more
> if real stars fell and lodged
> on my coat."
> —Henry David Thoreau, essayist,
> poet, and philosopher

Snowflakes, our snow physicist teaches us, are not perfectly
symmetrical. Check this out for yourself. The next time it snows,
go outside and catch some falling snowflakes, preferably on a
dark or brightly colored glove. Examine them closely. The beauti-
fully symmetrical ones are challenging to find, while the irregular
crystals are far more common. Nature is certainly true to form:
beauty belies perfect shapes and balanced symmetry.

In 1951 the International Commission on Snow and Ice produced a fairly simple and widely used classification system for
solid precipitation. This system defines the seven principal snow
crystal types as plates, stellar crystals, columns, needles, spatial
dendrites, capped columns, and irregular forms. Later, physicist
Ukichiro Nakaya created the first systematic classification
scheme for snowflakes, in which he subdivided falling snow into
forty-one individual morphological types. The most complex

classification scheme is an extension of Nakaya's table, published by meteorologists C. Magono and C. W. Lee in 1966. This table includes an astounding eighty different snow crystal types!

Which finally brings us to the age-old question: is it true that no two snowflakes are exactly alike? Libbrecht responds to the Zen-like quandary that the short answer to the question is yes—it is extremely improbable that two *complex* snowflakes will look *exactly* alike. So extremely improbable, in fact, that even if you looked at every flake ever created, you would not find any exactly alike. (In true scientific form, Libbrecht expresses that the long answer is a bit more involved—it depends on just what you mean by "alike" and on just what you mean by "snowflake." For more on Libbrecht's amazing work, visit his website, www.snowcrystals.com.)

Wow! Rather amazing, when you stop to consider it—how these intricate, diverse, labyrinthine structures of snowflakes emerge spontaneously, literally out of thin air, as they flitter and float through the clouds. It gives us pause, doesn't it? Creative brilliance has seen to it that even down to something as minute and seemingly insignificant as the snowflake, variations are their hallmark. Their very imperfections and uniqueness contribute to their beauty. How much we can learn from nature's designs! The magnitude of snowflakes' diversity mirrors our diversity in the human species. And yet, too often, it is the differences between us—skin color, religion, ethnicity, gender, class, family status—that cause us to treat one another harshly, allowing discrimination, conflict, and oppression to be our daily reality. The snowflakes seem to be teaching us to revel in our differences endowed by our Creator.

"When there's snow on the ground, I like to pretend I'm walking on clouds."
—from *Animal Crossing: Wild World* by Takayuki Ikkaku, Arisa Hosaka, and Toshihiro Kawabata

There you have it. Everything you wanted to know about snow but were afraid to ask. May you never ponder a snowflake the same way again. Or the night sky or darkness or winter or the cold. Be a bold winter adventurer! Spend some time in quiet reflection. Rekindle a connection with your own soul. Gift yourself with a few silent moments communing with a winter landscape, and let all of

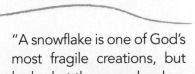

"A snowflake is one of God's most fragile creations, but look what they can do when they stick together!"

—Anonymous

your senses be roused and fully present. Allow the attributes that are uniquely winter to awaken your sense of awe. Let all the temporal deaths of the season pierce you, invigorate you, and bring you alive because you *feel*. Honor where your inner spaces long for the stillness you behold in frozen wilderness. Touch the deep places where the contours of the winterscape mirror the spiritual geography within. Craft your own outings that will wow you into experiencing the wonders of this amazing season.

❄ A *Reflective* Moment

The next time you're out on the slopes, in the woods, or even in your own backyard and it is snowing, stop and look intently at the flakes that land on your sleeve. Ponder how amazing it is that one, then two, then ten, then a hundred, then thousands of these tiny little particles, all different, end up covering mountain after mountain with multiple *feet* of snow. Copious amounts of snow that make skiing possible, that make snowboarding possible, that make all manner of snow sports possible, that in the spring make rivers flow and plants grow. Consider the link between the creativity in one flake, the beauty of the winter landscape, your pleasure in being out in it, and the thrill of the sport that these mysterious specks make possible. Feel your gratitude for this gift that is given *one snowflake at a time*.

Conversation with an Adventurer
Jamie Korngold, spiritual skiing guide
～

Rabbi Jamie Korngold is known as the "Adventure Rabbi." In 2001 she left traditional rabbinate and began to reconnect people with the spirituality of the great outdoors, and she now leads "spiritual skiing" retreats in the mountains of Colorado. We talked to her about these adventures.

What is the connection for you between "adventure" and "spirituality"?

Abraham Joshua Heschel, one of our great rabbis and thinkers, wrote, "God begins where words end." Similarly, for me, a spiritual quest involves getting to a place beyond words. For some of us, strenuous outdoor physical exercise—whether it is running, hiking, or skiing—can move us from thinking to just being. Creating a spiritual experience in these settings takes very little effort. I just have to crystallize or intentionalize what's already happening. I often think of the outdoors as a springboard for a spiritual experience.

You say in your book, *God in the Wilderness,* that our lives are already spiritual. When people come to you for "spiritual skiing" experiences, do they know they are yearning for something?

Our culture is frenetic. How often have you heard this conversation? You ask a friend, "How are you?" and she answers, "Good ... busy, but good." It has become a badge of courage to be busy. But despite all this running around, there are still myriad spiritual moments in our lives. What we need is someone or something to help us slow down and notice them.

One of my tasks as a spiritual leader and rabbi is to create speed bumps to help us slow down. In the Jewish tradition we say a blessing before we do many things, but there are many ways of creating pauses in our lives so we can notice the richness that already exists. When people finally reach the place of slowing down, even just a little, they are so relieved. It's like coming home.

On a ski retreat I led last winter, there was an intense workaholic who arrived late because he was still in the car sending text messages. He let us know early that he was not going to be at half the programs because he had to work. Yet three hours into the retreat, he got so into what we were doing that he put away all his work! His wife said she had not seen him so fully present in years.

Sometimes even going to the slopes can feel very busy, especially if you are a first-timer or are visiting a new mountain. What suggestions do you have for getting past the busyness of skiing?

I lead regular outdoor Sabbath services on top of Copper Mountain Ski Resort. A family from Ohio came to our service on the last day of their weeklong ski vacation. There is a prayer in the Jewish morning service in which we thank God for the beauty of creation. Rather than read the prayer, I asked everyone to stop and look around and notice something they wouldn't have noticed if I hadn't asked them. And so people pointed out snow crystals, the intense blue of the sky, formations of the snow, and so on. Four years after that service, the mother called me to talk about that service and her family's reaction to it. She said, "That was the first time all week we had stopped to look around. And we still remember that teaching!"

Are there things you invite people to do while they are on a run?

When I lead ski days, it is not about learning to ski; it is about *spiritual* skiing. I'll stop and offer a teaching, using a spiritual reading, while people catch their breath. Then I'll invite them to think about it as they are skiing down, and we talk about it at the next stop or while we are in the chair lift. As an example of a teaching, this is a Hasidic tale from Martin Buber that I like to share: The Rabbi of Kotzk asked some learned Jews who were visiting him, "Where does God dwell?" They laughed and replied, "What a thing to ask. God dwells everywhere, of course!" And then the Rabbi answered his own question: "God dwells where we let God in."

Or I'll invite people to think about this: Why were Christianity and Judaism created in the outdoors? Are there certain spiritual lessons that we get best when we are outside? Take Psalm 23. Why is it that God tells us that when we need comfort, we should go outside? "[God] makes me lie down in green pastures ... leads me beside still waters ... restores my soul" (Psalm 23:2–3). Why sit by a field? Why a lake? Just before people begin their next ski run, I'll suggest, "Think about why you find comfort here."

You speak of many outdoor activities as "spiritual portals" for us. Is there some way that being in the snow is unique as a spiritual entry point?

I think there is a unique quietness to it. The earth is at rest. There are some birds and a few mammals about, but not a lot. It inspires me to get into that mood, too, especially with snowshoeing or backcountry skiing. There is a quiet serenity that is covering the earth, inviting us to serenity as well.

5 Zapped into the Zone
Finding Your Kinesthetic Groove

THOUGHTS FROM MARCIA

IN THE BOOK *Flow: The Psychology of Optimal Experience*, psychology professor Mihaly Csikszentmihalyi describes the state in which people are so involved in an activity that nothing else seems to matter. This "optimal experience" comes on the occasion when "we feel a sense of exhilaration, a deep sense of enjoyment that is long cherished and that becomes a landmark in memory for what life should be like." The terms "groove" and "being in the Zone" have similar connotations. Musicians and athletes frequently use "groove" to express the experience of everything fitting just right. It is a place of rhythm that can sustain itself through time, seemingly without effort. The field of sports psychology is filled with studies and examples of "being in the Zone." Perhaps you've experienced that in winter sports— moments when the rhythm is so right that you enter a "Zone" where nothing else exists in the world.

If you haven't experienced the Zone on the mountain yet, there is probably some area of your life where you've caught at least a glimpse of this kind of "optimal experience." It might be in the rhythm of running five miles or in the utter concentration as you white-water raft in rushing rivers over boulders. It doesn't have to be a "wild ride" kind of experience, though. You could feel it while gently rocking an infant. The Zone has many rhythms and tempos. Whatever rhythm it is that you synchronize with or tune in to, when you settle into that pattern, it creates a feeling of "time-out-of-time." This "time out" is important to our spiritual well-being because it acts as relief from the relentless clock-watching time frames we normally find ourselves in. Finding a groove through physical activity is an essential part of our health, especially our mental and spiritual health.

Spiritual Epiphany

Religion literally means "to bind together." Since prehistoric ritual and religion began, humans have found ways to bind together as a group. In his study called *Keeping Together in Time*, William McNeill explores the ancient phenomenon of what he calls "muscular bonding." He believes that in the course of human history, *Homo sapiens* learned to physically "keep time together," which gave them a great evolutionary advantage. In their ritual dances around the fire, their common rhythm and motion helped them feel more power, contributed to their health, and offered preparation and energy for the hunting season. In their walking from place to place with songs and rhythmic stepping, they felt a sense of belonging to a whole along their journeys. With their songs, whether they were grinding corn or weaving fabric, they could work longer as the rhythms carried them along.

> "When the crystalline moment does approach, and time slows down and all becomes deliciously vivid around you, resist the temptation to retain or analyze your awareness. Just let it happen. Go with it, flow with it. Bathe in it joyfully. Without trying, you will understand it best."
> —Rick Phipps, *Skiing Zen*

These common kinesthetic (movement) experiences helped ancient peoples bond emotionally so that they had greater allegiance to one another, were able to gather larger and larger numbers together, and could band together more strongly to fight for survival. So the urge to find a groove with others and with our surroundings is deeply embedded in our genes. Our bodies just know how to do this, just as they know how to sweat without us telling them to sweat. We don't have to learn this; we just have to let it happen.

We come from a long line of evolutionary human history that equates motion and rhythm with spiritual experience. All kinds of traditional and ancient spiritual practices are rooted in rhythms. Pilgrims walking to Mecca, Jews rocking in prayer at the Wailing Wall, Christians walking a labyrinth, or Sufi dervishes whirling in circles—all are engaging in spiritual practices where the outward rhythmic activity makes an inward difference. Amazingly enough, no matter whether it is a slow or fast rhythm, people who do these things often find them-

> "In the beginning was noise. And noise begat rhythm. And rhythm begat everything else. And the dance began."
> —Mickey Hart of the Grateful Dead, *Drumming at the Edge of Magic*

selves in a place of heightened spiritual awareness. They might not call it a groove or a Zone, but essentially motion and rhythm brought them to that time-out-of-time place.

In *Skiing Zen*, Rick Phipps, writer, speaker, and entrepreneur, describes a moment when he is trying to make a decision about either going back to a Japanese monastery where he has been invited to be a disciple for a time or continuing toward his goal of skiing in the mountains of Japan. He visualizes both scenarios, first visiting in his mind's eye the intensity of the quiet calm of sitting and meditating at the monastery, then visualizing himself carving and swiveling down steep faces of the snowy mountains. He writes, "Strangely, the same emotion accompanied these disparate images. Though the first were of meditative isolation and the others were of rapid action, I felt a deep calm throughout." This phenomenon haunts him: "How can such different activities yield the same awareness?"

This is a strange phenomenon, yet it's true. Vastly different activities can yield similar results when we engage in them deeply enough. Neuroscientists have discovered that when the part of the nervous system that creates a high energy release is greatly stimulated, it can trigger simultaneous activity in the part of the nervous system that quiets us. So when Rick describes his "deep calm" in the midst of vigorous skiing, he is probably describing the simultaneous activity in his brain. It also works the other way around. In his intense meditation, that calming part of the brain is so stimulated that it causes the rapid-motion part of the brain to function as well, giving him super clarity and the sense of a tremendous energy rush, even though he is sitting still.

> "Skiing is a dance, and the mountain always leads."
> —Anonymous

Sometimes when we are concentrating with great intention *and* are engaged in intense repetitive rhythmic activity (such as skiing, riding, skating, or trekking), this stimulation of both of these systems in the brain happens. We feel energized and calm all at the same time. We feel powerful, and we feel at peace. Not a bad state of being! There is also another by-product of this that can occur: we can begin to feel oneness with everything. Why? Apparently, when there is so much activity in the brain, we have to inhibit activity in some parts in order to conserve energy for the parts of the brain where the super-buzz is going on. The parts of the brain that get the plug pulled for a time are places that enable us to know the boundaries between ourselves and everything else. When this happens, the boundaries between us and other people, between us and the snow and the trees, between us and our skis or board, disappear.

The places in the brain where we perceive time and space get minimized as well. With input to these functions reduced, we start to feel that we are literally a part of everything—a union of our bodies, the mountain, the sky, the motion. And we get that sense that time "stands still." Truly getting "zapped into the Zone" is often about particular synapses firing more than others and other nerve impulses shutting off, until we have what some call a "mountaintop experience."

So, in a sense, we can be a bit "out of our mind," or at least the activities of our bodies can alter the activity in our brains. Besides the epiphanies, or insights, that are possible when we consciously become aware of the sensations of our bodies, there is also the sensation of being *less* conscious of every little detail—the mind does a "letting go" in order to "let God," to use a proverbial phrase. We get in our own way sometimes when we overanalyze everything. Rhythmic activity can help us let loose. Have you ever "lost yourself" on the dance floor? Felt your cares "fall away" when a favorite song came on the radio? Came to the bottom of a ski run "before you knew it"?

"We can talk about, or around, the epiphanistic moment but, as spiritual leaders have said for centuries, you must experience it for yourself to truly understand."
—Rick Phipps, *Skiing Zen*

These time-out-of-time experiences are helped when we let go enough to become so engrossed in what we are doing that we stop thinking too much. The authors of *Inner Skiing* point out, "Much to our chagrin, breakthroughs in skiing or in any other activity virtually never happen when we plan them, and therefore they usually seem accidental. But they don't happen by chance." It's only when we can stop judging ourselves, stop analyzing whether or not we are doing it "right," and let go into the rhythm of our bodies in motion (no matter the speed) that we are rewarded with the kind of freedom that can lead to epiphany.

In case you're getting uncomfortable with this melding of spirituality and brain science—as if a spiritual experience could be boiled down to a few brain synapses—consider this: just because we know it is really our taste buds sending messages to the taste centers in our brains that help us perceive the deliciousness of a bowl of chocolate ice cream, it is *still* a real bowl of ice cream. Just because we know the physiological reasons why we have spiritual epiphanies, it still is a spiritual epiphany. We can still believe in something at work bigger than ourselves—the Divine in whatever names you use—even if we acknowledge that it is through these miraculously created bodies that we perceive this. I'm not trying to trump belief with proof here. I'm just trying to turn you on to an amazing phenomenon that points again to the essential connection between body, mind, and spirit—a connection that turns up the volume on spiritual awareness.

> "Nothing is more wondrous about the fifteen billion neurons in the human brain than their ability to convert thoughts, hopes, ideas, and attitudes into chemical substances. Everything begins, therefore, with belief. What we believe is the most powerful option of all."
>
> —Norman Cousins,
> *Anatomy of an Illness*

In the chapter on "the physicality of spirituality," I pointed out that our bodies are the only means by which we have any kind of experience. It just so happens that because we humans overthink everything, groan about the past and worry about the future so much, we need activities that help us suspend some of that to make room for an awareness of the present. Then we can be rejuvenated by these experiences of energy, calm, and the feeling of wholeness and something bigger than ourselves. They might last for only a short time, but their effects on our overall well-being are immense. These unforgettable moments become benchmarks by which we can claim and remember that we are part of something greater than ourselves, especially during times when pain and worry leave us feeling lonely or afraid.

Find Your Groove

What kind of rhythms get you into the Zone? Some of us more readily find our groove with strong, fast, linear bursts of energy. Others of us are more in sync with a lilting back-and-forth motion. Still others find a thrill and awe in a perfectly executed run in the halfpipe, while some just want to hang loose in the backcountry.

Our particular rhythms are part of a vast array of rhythms that constitute the created universe. If we could look through a high-powered microscope into our bodies at our innermost and perhaps tiniest subatomic level, we would see tiny quarks dancing in rhythmic relationship, creating a communication system that is an amazing dance of life within us. Even when we are still, we aren't still. The same is true of the desks or chairs or snowboards or skis. And if we could look into a high-powered telescope toward the outermost horizons of the universe, we would see an ever-expanding universe of stars and systems that also moves, at incredible

> "At the root of all power and motion, at the burning center of existence itself, there is music and rhythm, the play of patterned frequencies against the matrix of time."
>
> —George Leonard, pioneer in the field of human potential

velocities and distances, in great cosmic rhythms. All that exists is in motion, and we are each part of that picture, from the smallest to the grandest of the rhythms of life.

As you head down or across the mountain, there also exists a symphony of multiple rhythms. The rhythms that feel good to your particular body collaborate with the rhythms allowed by the equipment you use. There are also the rhythms demanded by the terrain itself and, finally, the rhythms of the world as it passes by you, depending on wind, velocity, snow conditions, and myriad other factors. W*hew*. If you thought about all this at once, you'd never find the Zone! That's why being able to forget all this stuff momentarily comes in handy for entering a groove that becomes a spiritual experience.

But knowing more about how rhythms work can help you understand more about how you can access spiritual experiences in your adventures in the snow or why certain adventures work for you and others just don't. The basic thing to know is that people don't all march to the beat of the same drummer. This means that there are certain grooves that will take you to those euphoric places of "flow" easier than others.

Take Karen and myself. We are good friends and also very, very different. My energy off the slopes can get pretty fast-paced, even frenetic, as I juggle out-of-town traveling and teaching and lots of projects. Karen juggles many things, too, but her energy off of her snowboard is much more laid-back and methodical as she cares for her young son and prepares sermons and retreats. But get us out there in the white stuff, and our alter egos seem to take over. We ride the lift together, and that seems to be the extent of our skiing and riding "together." I take my time drinking in the scene and indulging in lazy S curves down the hill, while Karen, as soon as she straps into her snowboard at the top, is off like a shot in an adrenaline race to the finish. Both forms are valid grooves. There is no one "right" way to ski or snowboard, whether downhill, cross country, or backcountry; we each have our own rhythms. Here's a bit more about what it's like for Karen and me:

Marcia's Love for 'Roy

Corduroy. Ah … a sunny morning, an early start, and freshly groomed "corduroy"—not the fabric, of course, but the freshly packed powder that's been combed until it looks like tiny farm furrows in a well-tended field. On it, I can sow the seeds of pure bliss. While some people "jones" for a powder day (where you glide through feathers of snow that part at your ankles), I am a sucker for corduroy. The big, wide swaths of smoothed-out terrain allow me to stop focusing on navigating bumps and chopped snow and, instead, focus on the "big picture"—my body's flight through space.

My favorite warm-up run at Northstar-at-Tahoe is called Logger's Loop. It was probably originally just what its name suggests—a long road that winds down in an easy decline, used by big logging trucks as they cleared timber on the mountain. I often abandon my skiing technique and schooled postures and simply let my "wings" unfurl at my sides, gliding down the run as if I'm one of the bald eagles we are occasionally privileged to see here. I always wear a helmet, so the "wind in the hair" experience is not one I indulge in, but on warm Tahoe days, I unzip my jacket so it will flap behind me, adding to a sense of flight.

> "Our bodies were meant to have that rhythm and grace ... everybody will have something they feel comfortable with or love to do. It's pretty important to have something like that in your life where you feel comfortable, like having fun flying down a hill."
>
> —Tina Basich, U.S. snowboarding champion

The other day I found a great run on Colorado's Winter Park slopes. It was just easy enough for me not to have to worry about the terrain, but steep enough to get fairly good speed while alternating between wide S curves and tighter turns. I opened my focus to include the vast Rockies that the wide run opened in front of me. This was it. The groove I was looking for was filled with ease and grandeur. This is what flips on the "joy switch" for me every time. I vowed to do this run until the bewitching hour when the lifts closed—and I did.

Karen's Need for Speed

I have a wintertime addiction: the weather channel. I am always on the lookout for the next storm. Will it bring snow measured in inches or in feet? I head out to the mountain as soon as the first few inches fall. If it's still coming down, all the better—bring on the powder. I can feel the "itch" deep inside my body all the way up the lift. With delicious anticipation bordering on antsy-ness, I am literally salivating. I feel like those dogsled canines who yip and whine and strain against their harnesses as soon as they sense it is almost time to go. I strap on my board at the top of Burnout and head down the backside. It has snowed so much all night that the "groomers" have cut only one swath down the center of several runs, what they call a "mercy pass." This leaves acres of awesome untracked powder to play in on the edges of the run. Allowing gravity to have its way, I let the powder up to my knees keep me going at a moderate speed. I carve subtle turns as I listen to the soft hiss of my board.

The next day I am back to hit some fresh groomers, again antsy in anticipation of the rush. I strap in at the top of Gully and point downhill. I dare myself not to turn. As I pick up speed, the endorphins start in my toes and flow upward right through the top of my head. I feel as if I am flying. I ditch anything that resembles proper form and crouch low on my board. I feel my speed increase. I push my heel-side edge out hard for a fast wide arc, then lean out for a toe-side carve. Again I crouch and pick up speed until I reach the slow zone near the lift. There is nothing in the world except me and my board and one glorious mountain. I can't stop smiling.

Honor Your Rhythm

Each of our bodies has a unique rhythm by which we move through the world. Did you know that even the breathing patterns of infants are different? That our basic brain waves are not all alike? Like the uniqueness of our fingerprints, we have patterns and rhythms that are varied. And our body rhythms are real and can be felt by others. "You have so much energy!" is a comment we say to someone when we feel the rhythm of their body and movement and are affected by it. Or we might notice that someone's normal energy is "off" and respond, "You don't seem like yourself today."

What all this points to is that part of who we are, part of our "spirit" of life, is tied to the patterns of our energy, the rhythms of our bodies. People's brains and muscles—the neuromuscular connections—do not all work with the same dynamics of energy. Some of us have brains that signal muscles to explode with a burst, while others have neurons that communicate a more laid-back tempo. One person goes to the ski resort mainly to relax in the spa, while another's idea of rejuvenation is a full-on day flying down every slope on the mountain until they close it down!

> "If today I want to go fast, I go fast; if tomorrow I want to go slow, I go slow. What we are fighting for is the right to determine our own tempos."
>
> —Carl Honoré, *In Praise of Slowness*

Through studying people in motion, researchers have come up with a theory that we each have a "home pattern." Of course, we don't always have the same energy throughout the day or throughout our lives. The rhythmic "frequencies" through which we experience the world vary depending on what needs to get accomplished. But our "home pattern" of rhythm and energy is how our bodies *want* to move, even what they *crave*. This is the rhythm that makes us feel most like ourselves. In the best sense of the word, a "home pattern" is one in which we find our greatest ease, where we can be most relaxed. It is also where we connect with our greatest power, where we have the most endurance. It is our particular groove. When we go for a long time without getting to live in our groove, we are not at home with ourselves. We feel depleted, and something feels "off."

Have you experienced that? This is what makes recognizing your groove so important to your spiritual life. You need to know when you are out of sync and which activities will help you get back in tune. It is important to give yourself permission to indulge in that groove and to see this as part of your spiritual nurture. Like a tuning fork, when we find activities that truly resonate within us, the reverberations last a good long while. Being spiritually tuned-in requires regular participation in those things that create life-giving reverberations that permeate our lives.

"While being in the Zone, this is where the projections of the mind are no longer experienced, where the body no longer feels, you move beyond both to become your true nature— who you truly are. This is why sport is so nourishing—as essential as food— for it has the potential to change your reality and bring you home."

—Kristen Ulmer, spiritual ski guide and extreme sports pioneer

So, while I *can* plummet down the slope and stay (somewhat) close to Karen whizzing down the hill (if she's going "slow"), I cannot keep that up for very long because it is beyond my technical ability; it drains my energy and my mental capacity. And neither would Karen enjoy a whole day of following my particular rhythms. She would literally be "itching" to get on with it! And you know what? It's totally okay.

Unless you are striving to be the fastest on skis or dying to grab the most air on a snowboard or make it to the Olympics, the point is to honor the rhythm that brings you the most joy. Because it is there, and only there, that you will be able to tune in to the Zone.

❅ A *Reflective* Moment

Just as different people have different life energies, the ways in which you find your bliss in winter activities will also be vastly different. Your groove on the slopes may be a *match* for your life energy or a *counterbalance* (as it is for Karen and me). As you ski or snowboard or snowshoe, try different rhythms with your motion. Notice which rhythms require you to think so much that you can't enjoy the moment. Notice when you aren't challenged enough and your mind starts to formulate your grocery list or some other "to-do" list. Draw your awareness back to your body, to the sounds of your equipment on the snow, to what makes you aware of your rhythms. If you usually have earphones feeding you music, try turning the music off so you can hear your own music. And if you never listen to music, try (on a less-crowded run) several kinds of music with varying rhythmic tempos to see what gives you the most exhilarating feeling. Different days may bring different responses for you. The point is to "tune in" and discover, for this moment, what renews your soul.

Now relate this to your spirit of life. What pace causes you stress in your life, and what pace seems to suit you? Perhaps you feel stuck and bored in a rhythm that has become monotonous or way too slow for you. It may be that your home rhythm, the groove that will feed you the most energy, needs to be more active. If something is bringing you down, feeling a rush may be just what your spirit needs to rejuvenate.

Or maybe the rhythms of your life are racing out of control and what you crave is some downtime. The interesting thing about rhythms is that a faster pace may not necessarily help you get more done. If your spirit gets depleted by speed, a slower pace is more likely to sustain your ease and help you do your best work—work that won't need to be undone or redone because you rushed through it. Just as some people will be drawn to a steep slope that propels them on a gravity ride of adrenaline, and others would be exhausted and shaking if they did that same thing, you need to find the tempo of life that nourishes you. And it is important not to judge yourself—or others—based on those differences.

Synchronicity

Our rhythms can have an effect on each other, just as the rhythms of the world around us can have an effect on us. So, as important as it is to pay attention to which grooves are uniquely ours, it is also essential to pay attention to the groove of the things surrounding us—our environment and our relationships. These powerful outside rhythms can help us or hurt us.

The law of entrainment is a law of physics that says that when two rhythms are nearly the same and they come into close proximity, they will "entrain," or lock up in synchrony. You may notice this when you are driving and the windshield wipers start beating to the rhythm of the music on the radio, if only for a few moments. Entrainment is what happens when people live together and their patterns of speech start to sound alike or they fall into similar rhythms of living.

For many years before I went to seminary, I was a professional dancer in New York City. I was a member of an eight-person dance company that performed together just about every day, traveling around the world. Audiences raved about our ability to synchronize our movements to such an extent that we looked like one organism at times. Although we spent a lot of time in rehearsal working on moving at the same exact moment with the same exact energy, in the moment of performance it was not about perfection, but more about riding on the energy wave of the group—an exciting experience that the audience could feel even in their seats.

> "The essence of the beautiful is unity in variety."
> —William Somerset Maugham, short-story writer, novelist, and playwright

When I try to ski in unison with someone else, I'm calling on my ability to synchronize with the other person's groove, just as I did in the dance company. Even though Karen and I don't ski and ride alike, there are times when I push myself to keep up with her because this is how I get better. I try to "sync-up" as much as I can with her speed and trajectory and literally feed off of it. Or, sometimes when I am skiing alone, I fall in behind someone who is skiing just ahead of me, turning when they turn, following their tracks, and mimicking their rhythms. It gives my body a challenge, and I find that I get a real shot of intense focusing and adrenaline, even if that person's pace is not so fast. The fun, and the rush, is in tuning in to another.

Ski instructors, too, often invite their students to engage in follow-the-leader so they can establish and encourage a particular rhythm. The power of rhythm and our bodies' abilities to synchronize can offer us encouragement to grow and reach beyond what we ourselves would try. Have you ever been hesitant to do something you've never done before, but the person you are with has such an infectious enthusiasm that you find yourself plunging ahead and then being so grateful that you did?

The spirit of adventure can be a thrilling thing to share, and it can also help us grow in ways we never imagined we could. This is one of the reasons adventure can enhance our spirituality. Our spiritual lives are not just something personal but are also connected with the people and communities of which we are a part. Deepening our spirituality requires an extension of ourselves. Learning to sync-up with

> "Snowboarding is an activity that is very popular with people who do not feel that regular skiing is lethal enough.... I now realize that the small hills you see on ski slopes are formed around the bodies of forty-seven-year-olds who tried to learn snowboarding."
>
> —Dave Barry, humor columnist

another's "e-motions" uses the same skills we use to sync-up with someone else's motion. We get to exercise our neurobiology of empathy, of identifying with someone else's life journey, which prepares us to be more compassionate human beings.

But just as our capacity to tune in can be helpful, it can also be harmful if we are not discerning about our limits. Following someone on the slopes who is way out of your league technically (or who is more concerned about other things than your needs) can get you into places that you shouldn't be. As a kid learning to ski, I can remember my brother taking me on the Drunken Frenchman black-diamond run at Winter Park after much pleading to follow him on this "cool run." In those days there was no such thing as snowboarding or terrain parks, and Jeff would build his own jumps on the sides of the runs. Ski patrol would follow kids like my brother around and destroy these homemade jumps. (It just irks him to no end that, today, when his football-playing knees are creaky and can't take the landings, resorts spend tons of time and money making jumps!) Anyway, as you might imagine, I ended up sliding on my butt most of the way down the Drunken Frenchman. He, in the meantime, was off in the trees hotdogging it to his heart's content.

Now, we were kids and this is what happens sometimes with siblings. No harm was meant, and it gives us a good story to laugh about now. But when I reflect on a deeper level about this experience, I can also see how this instance was a glimpse into what would be some unfortunate following of other people in my life into directions that were not "me." My need to please, to be liked, and a fear of rejection clouded my decisions about which rhythms I should have been wary about following.

How many countless people have headed for mountain ski runs that were beyond their capacity just so they wouldn't be seen as "less than," feel embarrassed in front of their friends, or be perceived as a wimp? There is a fine line between pushing ourselves and knowing ourselves, our limits, and our true desires. In life, as in our adventures in the snow, paying attention to and honoring the rhythms of our bodies, of our lives, and of our relationships are essential.

Let your adventures in the snow help you reflect on the grooves of your life, the rhythms of your movement on this earth, so that you can live to *your* fullest, not someone else's idea of who you should be. This is what it is to be "zapped into a Zone" that is spiritually optimal for you.

Conversation with an Adventurer
Neil Elliot, "soulriding" researcher

～

Neil Elliot is an Anglican priest and an avid snowboarder who has done doctoral research on "soulriding," a term that is used in a variety of ways in snowboarding, surfing, and mountain biking culture. He interviewed many snowboarders about their experiences, leading to what Neil calls "elements" of soulriding, which include play, freedom, rhythm, flow, risk, and community, among others. We talked to him about his own experience of skiing and snowboarding, and what he heard from the boarders he interviewed.

When did you first hear the term "soulriding"?

I don't remember when I actually heard it the first time. There was an e-mail group I was part of, and the conversation went to "out-of-body" experiences while riding. I could relate because there had been a few times, really riding pitches of powder, when I completely lost where I was. You get into it and you're flowing with it and you are kind of there and not there, in the body and not in the body. And so I threw this out for conversation, and a number of people began talking about the same kind of thing. Then somewhere in a magazine I came across the term "soulriding," and I wondered, "What's that about and how does it connect with this kind of out-of-body experience and what does it say about the potential link between spirituality and snowboarding?" So I started talking to people about that and started thinking, this would be a perfect piece of research—and a perfect excuse to do some riding!

When does snowboarding become "soulriding" or recreation become "something more"?

For me, soulriding is about an approach to snowboarding. It is about consciously connecting with something bigger than me in a variety of ways. But I also think there is more to it than that. From my interviews, I came up with ten different elements that are potential elements of spirituality, that contribute to the "something more" experience. Some are about experiences of "the other," and some are about developing the self—who I am, what community I am a part of, how I identify with a lifestyle that is not like everyone else. We are each trying to work out who we are. Some of the boarders I talked with said, "If you really want to know who I am, I'm a snow-boarder. I do other things, but at the heart, I am a snowboarder."

How did the people you interviewed describe "soulriding"?

This is not easy stuff to communicate. There is something incom-municable about the nature of spiritual experience. For some, soulriding is about being in the moment, just being completely engaged, completely there, in the Zone. That is where soulriding becomes an opportunity to learn. It takes you to that place, and then you begin to wonder how you do that in the rest of your life. How do I do this when I'm sitting at my desk? When I'm on my bike? When life isn't going so good? How do I find this again?

Did the snowboarders you interviewed connect their "in-the-Zone" experiences to spirituality?

Many people don't connect it to "God," but there is a connection to something "other"—however you describe that. It is part of a journey. Gen Xers seem to make the connection between spiritu-ality and physicality more easily than boomers do. And I think Eastern religions have had an impact on Western society that has enabled us to take on a whole new vocabulary of spirituality. So physicality is back on the agenda; attentiveness is on the agenda.

Are there practices or rituals that help get people "tuned-in" to the Zone?

The community is a significant part of that. For some people, it is being with others, and for some it is getting away from others. It just depends. But to be a part of a community of people who seek the experience usually seems to be important. Another thing is attitude. There is no such thing as bad snow, just bad approaches to the snow you've got.

In terms of rituals, most people might not see the little things they do in the morning to get ready to go to the mountain as important rituals. But actually getting to the top of the ski lift is the climax of a whole bunch of rituals that get you ready for being there. And then on the lift, some people chat or listen to music to get ramped up.

One of your ten elements of "soulriding" is a sense of "play." Tell us more about that.

Snowboarding has always been about play. It has connections with skateboarding ... you are not "perfecting a technique." The attitude is more about goofing off with your mates. It is about play. And the people I interviewed didn't see that as being something superficial. There is almost a sense that we are not allowed to play as adults, and this is a way to defy that. The idea is that play is time out of reality, out of the other things that we do. Both of these are references to being "in the Zone."

What about the element of "rhythm and flow" in "soulriding"?

Snowboarding is an edge-to-edge experience ... the rhythm is there. As you get better, the whole experience becomes one of flowing with the board, with the mountain. There were some people I talked to who distinguished between "tech riders" and "soulriders." Mostly, they described "tech riders" as people who just do the "point and shoot" and don't really see it as a spiritual thing. There is a sadness about them, as if they know they are missing something, but they can't really help themselves. They get going and "bang!" they are going to go as fast as they can or go off the biggest hit they can find. It's as if they learned one way of being on the hill, and while they know there are other ways of being, they can't bring themselves to go there.

But other people use a variety of different rhythms in their riding. Some think it is all about big powder turns, and others are quite happy to be carving up a groomer. They get to that same place "in the Zone" but in different ways. One of my best days this year was skiing short-radius turns where the whole thing was really flowing, getting really beautiful, weightless moments on a blue-black run. It was lovely. It's all about learning how to use the rhythm, the freedom of moving from one rhythm to another.

In your writing, you talk about how the mountains have inspired feelings of awe for as long as we have records, such as the accounts of Moses in the Hebrew Bible. "Soulriders," you say, are people who are aware of the sky, the mountains, the graceful and dramatic shapes, the whole environment in which they ride.

Somebody talking about soulriding said, "Some people go to the mountain to snowboard; others snowboard to go to the mountain." That really hits it! Just being in the mountains does something for my soul. It is not a matter of what I'm doing, but a matter of that which is worship, and being, and all kinds of spirituality coming together and happening at once. My mum is a psychotherapist, and one of the first questions she asks new clients is "What makes your soul sing?" And just being in the mountains is the one for me.

6 *More Than Buckling Up*

Tuning Awareness
beyond the Technical

THOUGHTS FROM MARCIA

PREPARING TO HIT THE SLOPES can be a daunting exercise for new adventurers. By the time you layer on, zip up, buckle down, and strap in, you're likely to be sweating and exhausted. But from experience, snow sport enthusiasts know that skiing on equipment that isn't tuned and waxed or doesn't fit well is like going for a run in flip-flops. It might work out okay, but it won't bring out your best or result in one of your top-ten snow days. And it might lead to serious frustration or even injury. The need for physical preparation is pretty clear, but what is the essential preparation for amazing *spiritual* adventures in the snow?

Whether it is your first day or five hundredth, tuning in and dialing up your awareness are as important as tuning up equipment. The first step is to recognize the importance of preparation. Karen and I recently had an experience that taught us a lot about what goes on behind the scenes to prepare the trails on which we later soar.

Preparation—A Story

If I'm driving at night on the road home, I can see the big snowcats that groom late at night moving up and down on the slopes I ski at Northstar-at-Tahoe Resort. I can't actually see those mammoth machines, but I can see their headlights ascending and descending like strange shooting stars in slow motion. I often wonder what it is like to be on the mountain at night, farming the snow into beautiful rows, smoothing the tracks of that day's revelers. I wonder what animals these groomers see peeping out after everyone has gone home—animals that live and sleep burrowed deep into the snow as we whiz by them by day. I wonder if the solitude on the hill in the darkness is enchanting, thrilling, or simply monotonous. So Karen and I decided to see if we could find out. Are there extra seats and would they let us ride one night?

> "How lucky are we to be one of relatively few people who have the privilege of being out playing on the mountain runs in these big machines in the middle of the night, seeing what no one else gets to see?"
> —Dave Myers, snowcat operator

Well, it helps to say you are writing a book. Once the director of operations talked to the head of media and PR, and then to the grooming staff, we were on! We arrived for the graveyard shift just before midnight to meet Sarah, the supervisor of grooming. To say that she is one of the most enthralled people with her job I've ever met would be an understatement. She is an impressive phenomenon behind the controls of the giant machine, but it isn't just about the machine for her. Although she has a degree in ski area management, neither is it just about "managing" the mountain. She likes—no, *loves*—to leave a cut-up trail completely smooth with that corduroy I adore, but when it comes down to it, her passion for the job is not simply about the technique of grooming. It is about the *experience*—the experience of being on the mountain in the dark of night, seeing what no one else sees, feeling the motion of the task at hand, witnessing the daily sunrise from the summit, being a part of the creation of beauty. We have dubbed her a "priestess" readying the outdoor "sanctuary" for the "ritual" of flying-down-the-slopes. Her vigil through the night, and the vigil of all the others who make the trek back and forth, up and down, night after night, is like combing the hair of the Mama Mountain so that when the light begins to dawn on her Spectacular Face, we can be awed again by the beauty on which we are about to tread.

As we start out with Sarah, she tunes her satellite radio to her favorite station for farming snow: movie soundtracks. The snowcat crawls up a black-diamond expert run that I have often gazed upon from the chair lift during the day with awe and horror because of its steep pitch. But we lay the very first pattern of corduroy on the way up as if it isn't steep at all. We get to the top and turn the big snowcat around. At the summit of the mountain, Sarah turns all the snowcat's eyes (lights) off so our eyes can adjust for a moment. We see the terrain in the almost-full moonlight. It feels as if we are truly a cat, sitting curled up on the top of our perch surveying the territory below with our night-eyes. Sarah points out the lights of the town in the distance, and then we fall silent for a time—except for the soundtrack. The score to the movie *Transformers* has begun on the radio. Oh, my. Imagine plaintive violin over low and long bass, then an expansive crescendo. The mood of the music gives the sweeping panorama before us extra drama.

> "We do our best spiritual work when we are just a little off balance."
>
> —John Winn, minister and spiritual mentor

Just then, the soundtrack segues in mood, and a thundering drum pulse begins, matching my heart rate. Right on cue Sarah shifts into gear and turns on our headlights, and we inch toward the precipice of the black-diamond Grouse Alley run. She informs us that this run is usually groomed with a winch secured to a tree or post, hooked onto the snowcat, which keeps it from careening down the steep slope as it grooms on the way down and then pulls it back up. But "The Beast"—a new demo snowcat this year—is bigger, with more horsepower, and so we are "freeriding" this slope with no tether. Sarah warns us that we might feel some sliding. "Oh, that's just great," I nervously think to myself. We top the crest, and the machine tilts down … and down … and … "Holy moley!" is the only dialogue I can muster. Not such an eloquent comment for such a dramatic moment. I'm sure I'm not the first one to have such an initial reaction to this tilt-a-whirl experience. Seriously, if I hadn't pushed my feet against the frame of the window in front of me, I'd have looked like a bug smashed on the windshield from the inside! I remember why going down this slope on skis is daunting.

Well, I get used to it. The snowcat is as sure on its feet as any feline I know, and I begin to trust that I will come out of this alive. And then I begin to truly enjoy it. I can see why Sarah is so passionate about taming these massive amounts of snow.

> "Through sports, if you pay attention and not miss the lessons, you can be powerful beyond measure. You can access and express the connection of everyone, and everything that exists."
> —Kristen Ulmer, spiritual ski guide and extreme sports pioneer

As she puts it, "It's a whole different perspective on the mountain. Groomers know things about the trees, the runs, the terrain that no one else knows or notices. You see things that other people never see—certain perspectives like going *up* the mountain. And the sunrises! The sunrises are it. They are the most spiritual part of my life. That is the moment I feel a connection to something Higher, God, or whatever you want to call it. It is my 'little sanctuary.'"

Just hours later, when skiers and riders show up, they will be, for the most part, oblivious to the hours of snow-farming preparation on their behalf. We so often focus on the obvious operations that we can see during the day as the elements that contribute to our adventures in the snow. But more often it is what happens "behind the scenes" that makes the difference. Our adventure of grooming the slopes with Sarah opened our eyes anew to the importance of preparation.

Knowing that the mountain has been so lovingly prepared for you, how will you prepare for the mountain? What spiritual equipment needs to be tuned so that you can make the most of your spiritual adventure? Reflecting on these questions before you hit the slopes, as well as in the midst of your adven-

"I realized that the way I had been skiing was a reflection on my life. Everything was done in a rush; I worked, came home, changed clothes, and went out again. I thought I had to move fast or I'd be left behind."

—Robert Kriegel, *Inner Skiing*

tures, can be a way of fine-tuning your mindset, or attitude, to see the connections between how you ski and how you live. This kind of reflecting creates the possibility that your attitudes on the slopes will positively affect your work and relationships, deepening your spiritual journey.

Tuning Your Presence

I am busy. I grew up with the idea that to be busy was evidence that you were living a valuable life—you were getting things done, accomplishing things. I'm not alone in this. It characterizes much of the North American work ethic, and especially that of the midwestern farm country where I was raised. I am constantly thinking one step ahead: "What is next on my 'to-do' list?" Subconsciously, I ask myself, "How can I accomplish an astonishing quantity today?" always somehow believing that getting copious amounts of work done will provide an opportunity to slow down tomorrow—only to find that tomorrow I end up repeating the same vicious cycle. This preoccupation with getting things done means that I tend to live in the future more than live fully present today.

One of the reasons why skiing has become my spiritual practice is because I am never more fully present in the moment than when I am on the mountain, the wind in my face, the intimate feel of my feet gliding over the earth. My "to-do" list is put away. My mind is not wandering around in next week somewhere, because the absolute delight of *right now* is not to be missed. This is freedom for me.

One of my favorite books in the past few years has been *In Praise of Slowness: Challenging the Cult of Speed* by Canadian journalist Carl Honoré. In it he describes the tyranny of speed: fast lives, fast food, fast relationships. "Tempted and titillated at every turn, we seek to cram in as much consumption and as many experiences as possible." He names some of those things we try to cram in in one life: careers, learning courses, working out, reading the paper, playing sports, going out with friends and family, watching TV, listening to music, vacations, and volunteer work. "The result is a gnawing disconnect between what we want from life and the sense that there is never enough time."

> "You have enough. You do enough. You are enough."
> —Sark, *Inspiration Sandwich*

Even our "downtime" can become filled with expectations and anxiety over getting in all the things we want to experience. Many enthusiasts spend thousands of dollars on a ski vacation only to realize at week's end that they are just beginning to decompress from their hectic lives and fully "arrive." One of the things that struck me about being in that big snowcat with Sarah was that it takes time, and careful attention, to make those passes until the whole run is smoothed. And there is nothing else more important in that moment, in the middle of the dark night, than getting it just right. As Sarah says, "It is so satisfying to be smoothing over what we call 'dirty' snow—the cut-up snow from the day of skiers and riders—and turning it into 'clean' snow. I pay attention to the little things and go back over something that came out rough. There is a satisfaction in 'leaving it clean'—putting it 'to bed,' as we say."

Sometimes I yearn for the ability to focus my attention like that, to have the gift of reveling in one task, one moment, one purpose—like Sarah, leaving one thing "clean." And then I hear the voice of one of my favorite TV characters, Captain Jean-Luc Picard of the Starship Enterprise, saying, "Make it so!" It hits me that I am the only one who can decide to do it, to be fully present in the moment, to give myself permission to renew my soul by setting aside the incessant need for "more-than-this."

Tuning in to the present moment is to become absorbed in what we are doing. When we are on the mountain, the benefits of doing this are somewhat cyclical: our spirit is renewed as we let go of the crowded lives we usually lead, *and* we become better skiers and riders as well, which in turn allows us more delight in the moment. If we diffuse our attention, as we so often do in our busy lives, we are in for a less-than-optimal experience. We won't be in touch with what our bodies are telling us and what the terrain is offering us in the moment. We will miss the opportunity to let it all come together, deepening our experience of flow.

> "When I concentrate so, the world disappears.... To ski a very steep slope is completely beautiful; it is pure, hard, vertical, luminous in a dimension that, by its nature, is foreign to us, yet I become a part of this cosmic dimension."
>
> —Patrick Vallencant, French alpine skier and pioneer in ski mountaineering

Absorption is about being "steeped" in something, soaking in it rather than striving for it. It is a kind of concentration that is relaxed but engaged. This is the preferred kind of "paying attention" for snow sports; say the authors of *Inner Skiing*. Rather than concentrating on *trying* to concentrate, we can pay attention by "focusing the light of awareness" in a particular direction, like shining a beam of light in order to see something better. This kind of easy concentration, or absorption in the moment, is often what leads to that feeling of "being in the Zone" or, as Neil Elliot (see the "Conversation with an Adventurer" at the end of chapter 5) described, "soulriding." One of the elements of soulriding, he says, is "transcendence." These moments of bliss can be like a meditation, where everything else falls away but the present. A common characteristic for those who describe this experience is the ability to let all cares, worries, and concerns take a break.

When I think about engaging in this practice of tuning my presence on the slopes, I also know that I can apply this principle to the rest of my life, offering myself the opportunity to create flow in all corners of my existence. Before you head for the slopes, begin to notice how much you are attempting to cram into one moment. Our society gives big points for multitasking, and at times life circumstances require it. But the mountain requires only your presence. Like putting a layer of wax on your skis or board for easier gliding, add a layer of permission for yourself to slow down, creating more ease for awhile. Who knows ... you may begin to offer yourself permission off the mountain as well.

Tuning Your Intentions

A well-groomed trail is not just about what the snow is like on the surface. The snowcat churns and tills the snow underneath its big body so that it is ready, or "conditioned," to be smoothed by the implements on the back of the machine. In fact, Sarah told us that "the most important aspect is the blade in the front of the machine. Learning to get that right, the right depth depending on the condition of the snow, using it to fill in the holes or move the snow to create a smoother surface—all that takes a while to learn. It's also amazing how much we have to destroy in order to create something new. The tilling of the snow, chopping it up, gives it back some air so it can be made into a much finer substance for grooming."

We are often disturbed by the churning up of our lives by conflict or change, sorrow or differences of opinion and perspective. But what if we could see these turbulent events as opportunities to touch something deeper in our spiritual journeys? What if we could recognize these as times when things buried under a beaten-down crusty layer have a chance to reveal themselves, offering us new surfaces on which to make fresh tracks? Awareness starts with noticing what lies under our hard-packed protective layers, but the next step is to hold whatever we discover with an easy intention that can open doors of understanding.

> "Inside all of us is a mountain with no top and no bottom.... Skiing this inner mountain has the power to satisfy the human longing to know oneself and the reason for which one was born."
> —W. Timothy Gallwey, *Inner Skiing*

In *Walking a Sacred Path: Rediscovering the Labyrinth as a Spiritual Tool*, Lauren Artress, founder of Veriditas, the World-Wide Labyrinth Project, describes how we can use our whole bodies as a spiritual practice. Walking a complex path can help focus us in ways that sensitize us, educate us, and help us discern thoughts that come from a "soul level" that we long to hear. The physicality imparts a focus and a peace in the midst of troubled feelings. "We can," Artress suggests, "strengthen ourselves by shedding tears, feeling the anger and hurt that keep us from experiencing our soul level. We can decide that we have held on to revenge too long, and take action to heal our hateful feelings. We can reconcile ourselves."

I have often experienced being on the mountain as a way of allowing feelings that live under the surface to get worked out. I have found that naming an intention before I do a run is an especially good way to open up avenues for transformation. Doing an activity with intent is a way of inviting a different kind of "know-ing," of coming to an understanding about something that lies under the surface, or of gaining wisdom about a difficult life moment. Sometimes I name an intention before I get to the mountain, and other times it comes to me in the midst of my day.

At Copper Mountain in Colorado, there is a beautiful out-door chapel on the slopes. I stopped there one heavenly pow-dery day at almost quitting time. So much snow had fallen in the previous couple of days that the chapel was frosted and glinting in the afternoon sun that had just peeked out for a minute. The chapel had not been dug out enough to actually go in, so I was just standing there for a bit, contemplating how transforming it could be for some churchgoers to be sitting in church up to their waists in sparkling white fluff, when one of the ambassadors of the resort skied up to me.

"Ah," he said, "you're making this stop, too. I'm just taking a moment to thank my great-grandma Nita for being in my life." His name tag indicated he was from Sydney, Australia. Then he added, "They are having her funeral right now in Sydney. I just needed to take a moment to say thanks."

"I'm so sorry," I said, and he quickly told me that it was all right, since she had eighty-nine feisty years—really good ones.

"I'm going to do this run for her—and for me."

The moment took me back to a couple of years ago when my cell phone rang just as I was getting off a lift at my home resort in Tahoe. It was my uncle, and he was trying to find my father because my beloved aunt Jeniel, who had been battling cancer, had passed away just moments before. Jeniel was my favorite aunt. She had been a champion ballroom dancer and had nur-tured my love of dance right into my professional career. She'd had a feisty seventy-something years, but I felt sure she'd been robbed of a lot more. I had struggled with my uneasy feelings around dying and death as I had watched her decline. Here I was just about to make one of my favorite runs, but the joy had been sucked right out of me. I sat there on one of the benches while various snowboarders glared at me, a skier who was hogging their space. So even though I didn't feel ready for it, I breathed a deep breath, whispered a quick "this one is for Jeniel," and took off down the run.

And then an image came to me: Movement. Spirit. Whooshing. Flying. Buzzing. Somehow the image of lifelessness in me was graciously replaced by quite the opposite, shifting from "the end" to "endless," from decay to rising, from pain to passion. And in that moment I realized that I was in the most perfect place to have heard this news about my beloved aunt. My whisper turned to a shout, "Let's do it, Jeniel!" and I had one of the most joyous runs ever, even with tears streaming and pooling in my goggles.

I'm quite sure my aunt never donned a pair of skis. But I knew at that moment that her indelible, adventurous spirit would always be part of my experiences on skis, and a part of my peacefulness about death.

> "Sometimes your joy is the source of your smile, but sometimes your smile can be the source of your joy."
> —Thich Nhat Hanh, Vietnamese monk, activist, and writer

It will still be difficult to understand the complexities about life-after-death, but I will always imagine that the feeling of flying, gliding, moving effortlessly through time and space as somehow close to the boundless freedom of "whatever's next." This knowing is something I gained from allowing myself an intentional run "for Jeniel."

Making your trips to the slopes and trails an intentional, deeper experience might include focusing on the spiritual life issues that you would like more wisdom about. Or you might focus on something you are dealing with, on life questions. What stuck places could benefit from an intentional focus during your spiritual adventure in the snow? Simply naming and tuning in to your questions before you start down the slope or out on the trail can create opportunities for breakthrough moments of deeper understanding. These intentions need not turn your attention away from fun, but they can percolate just beneath the surface. What your body reveals to you might surprise you.

Tuning Your Courage

Tuning in beyond the technical is also about tuning in to courage. Some of you reading this book may be preparing for your first-ever ski or snowboard adventure. You are probably aware that there will be fear involved the first time you look down from the top of a slope to the bottom, even if it is the bunny hill. But you know what? Even for experts, there is often fear involved. "Good" fear, as opposed to the debilitating kind of fear, is the body's natural way of helping us pay attention. In fact, fear is something we've needed throughout human history in order to stay alive. And I will venture to say that fear, as well as mustering courage, is also a part of being on a spiritual adventure.

"To begin a scary task is to be close to finishing it. In fact, beginning takes more courage than anything else, because once you make contact with the forces of nature, your most practical and clear-eyed self emerges."

—Lisa Jones, *Broken*

I remember the first time I attempted a black-diamond slope. At the top of it, I was almost frozen with the idea that I'd be heading down a slope that was *that* steep. I looked toward the distant bottom of the trail and felt it would take an eternity, because I just knew I'd be crisscrossing this hill at a snail's pace. I was hoping no one else was around, because I was sure that I would look totally uncool, wobbly, and scared. Even in my new favorite ski fashion, I was about to be the laughingstock of the hill.

My heart was racing, and I thought, "Thank God for the goggles!" because my eyes were bugging out and the expression on my face was giving away every ounce of fear.

I took the plunge. At the first or second turn, I thought, "Holy cow! Why did I do this?" I looked back, and it was too late, too far to sidestep my way back up. But then I began to breathe deeply, mustering courage, focusing on one turn at a time. I began to form a mantra in my mind, reminding myself of all I had learned about moving through difficult terrain. And bit by bit, I made my way to the bottom. Elation! I did it! I may have looked ridiculous and felt like I was going to die, but I had made it. And then I couldn't believe myself ... I actually began to formulate the notion of doing it *again*.

Sometimes the greatest feeling of accomplishment comes from taking the greatest risk. But, just as a good instructor would never encourage a beginner to skip the intermediate runs and head straight for the expert runs, chutes, and drop-offs, it is probably not a good idea to push yourself off the edge of something in your life that you haven't taken steps to prepare and train for. Part of spiritual adventure is knowing yourself and your limits and then going about the steps of learning new things in order to push those limits, accessing new discoveries.

The journey of the word "adventure" is an interesting one. Its beginnings in Olde English in the thirteenth century were simple: "adventure" originally meant "a thing about to happen," as well as "to come" or "to arrive." However, by the fourteenth century, the word had gained particular connotations, shifting to mean an inherently "risky or perilous undertaking." This was associated with daring and, of course, with courage to meet such a daring moment. In another couple of centuries, there was a

> "It's not your aptitude, but your attitude that will determine your altitude."
> —Anonymous

slight move again to meaning "a novel or exciting event." Rather than inferring that anything adventurous was "perilous," "adventure" took on the connotation of experiencing something new, something that was thrilling and exhilarating.

Certainly the adventures of winter sports carry both the risk and the excitement of this word's history. For this reason, our adventures in winter sports can be wonderful instruction for the adventures of our spiritual lives.

❄ A *Reflective Moment*

Whether you are a novice or a veteran of the slopes, as you prepare for your next adventure in the snow, reflect on how you deal with fear when faced with a new challenge in your life. Is the perceived perilous nature of the moment likely to paralyze you? Or are you able to focus your attention, see the next step, and then the next, and eventually move to a place of seeing the challenge as an exciting chance to grow and press through what were previous barriers in the journeys of your life? How might your experience on the slopes help you deal with fear in life situations?

Ski instructor Alex Heyman (see the "Conversation with an Adventurer" at the end of chapter 2) tells the story of teaching a woman who was very afraid. Because of her fear, she was skiing very slowly. Alex could tell that she was technically proficient enough to go much faster, but she just couldn't relax enough to allow more freedom in her skiing—which was hurting her spirit and curbing her joy. So Alex asked her to growl every time she made a turn. Initially, all she would do was a wimpy little "Grr," so he said, "Come on!" and demonstrated how he wanted her to really growl: "GRRRRR!" She felt embarrassed and uncomfortable making these silly noises, but Alex continued to encourage her. Finally, she started really growling, and then she started laughing … and skiing more aggressively with less fear.

Part of Alex's goal was to get her thinking about something other than fear, to get her focused on accomplishing a task that would offer her mind a different focus. His suggestion and encouragement to growl gave her permission to assert herself, to be more aggressive, and to ski to her full capacity.

When we are performing at our full capacity, we tap into our joy, our passion, our full sense of worth, and our own agency in

> "We should come home from adventures, and perils, and discoveries every day with new experience and character."
> —Henry David Thoreau, essayist, poet, and philosopher

the world. Meeting challenges on the mountain can be a spiritual opportunity to reflect on other challenges in our lives, perhaps on places where we are holding back because of fear.

Fear can be debilitating, I know. Although I haven't felt the paralysis of fear on the slopes for a while, I have experienced it in rock climbing a couple of times. For more than a few moments, I was convinced that there was nowhere to go, nothing I could do. I felt completely helpless and hopeless. Sometimes we describe moments like this as "fear got the better of me." This can be literally true. When we are overcome by fear, we may lose our best ability to see and sense which resources are at our disposal to get us out of a jam. When we see through the eyes of terror, some things become exaggerated. A steep slope may look and feel impossible. Looking at the entire slope all the way to the bottom may convince us that there is no end in sight. The courage to move ahead comes when we can tune our aware-

> "Awareness can focus on fear without fear. When we identify with fear we are afraid; when we identify with awareness we are that which is looking at the fear."
> —Robert Kriegel, *Inner Skiing*

ness to what *is* possible in the moment and train our attention only on what the next step is, rather than trying to deal with the overwhelming whole. Being able to shift from fear to one step forward is a valuable tool. It can help us get unstuck not only on the slopes but also in the turbulent times in our lives.

Champion snowboarder Tina Basich (see the "Conversation with an Adventurer" at the end of chapter 8) talks about what it was like for her when she returned to the slopes after an injury, only to find that the mental recovery was much more difficult than the physical recovery. "I could feel my ankle. It was a constant reminder of what happened, and I could feel the fear." Even though part of her never wanted to jump off anything again, part of her couldn't imagine never jumping again. She began to visualize successful jumps from her past to regain courage. She says, "I dug deep to my love for it, and it was my past experiences that brought me up to that present moment."

The root of the word "courage" is "heart." Before you hit the slopes or trails, take a moment to tune in to what is in your heart. Take heart, take a deep breath, know yourself as courageous, and rely on the wisdom and encouragement of others. Transforming an ordinary day on the mountain into a spiritual quest requires only this moment of preparation—moving your awareness beyond the technical aspects of what you are going to do into full attention, intention, and courage. This is the opening into a soul-full adventure.

Conversation with an Adventurer

Kristen Ulmer, extreme skier and spiritual teacher

～

For twelve years Kristen Ulmer was voted or named the best overall woman skier and the best big mountain extreme skier in the world. A pioneer of the extreme sports revolution, she went from U.S. Ski Team mogul specialist to jumping off cliffs and skiing "you-fall-you-die" ski descents around the world. In 2003 Kristen changed her life course and teamed up with Zen Master Genpo Roshi, in her home state of Utah, to offer clinics called "Ski to Live," which bring ancient wisdom into skiing and other adventures.

One of the participants in your "Ski to Live" events said, "These experiences are like fresh air in a smog-filled world." What do you find people are hungry for?
I find that people are looking for some sort of spiritual practice. I read somewhere that 93 percent of people say they are spiritual, but only a third of those say they are religious. So there is a hunger for spirituality, but many people don't know where to go. Often people are embarrassed to tell their friends they are going to a "spiritual" event, but coming to a ski clinic as an option is great. People know that something goes on in the mountains, they feel it, but they might not know how to tap into it.

You were a pioneer of extreme sports, taking huge risks and doing amazing feats. Now you invite others to do the same—in terms of growing within and knowing themselves. What is it like to be coaching people in these leaps in their lives?
Well, it is kind of like Michelangelo carving David. When he was asked, "How do you do this? How do you know what to do?" he said, "David is already existing in the stone, and it is up to me to

unleash him." I'm not teaching anything. I'm just here to help people unlock their own wisdom, to help them have access to something they might not otherwise have access to. I get so much out of it, too. Just being able to have another experience of the Absolute and share that with others in the beauty of nature, while in physical movement, is incredible. It is the coolest thing I've ever done in my life.

We often separate spirituality from physicality and separate wisdom from our bodies. Is it important that we put these things back together?

I think it is absolutely mandatory. The mind is a beautiful tool, but it is a terrible master. People say sports are 90 percent mental and the other 10 percent is mental, too! But actually, in sports done at the highest level, there is no thought. But we first have to congratulate the brain for doing its work, and then we can rely on the body. The body intuitively knows. It has a different kind of wisdom and consciousness—a consciousness that a lot of people don't get to experience. Most people build a shrine to the mind; it is who they are, it is what they are, end of story. But people who are involved in athletics that are very kinesthetic also know a different kind of wisdom. I'm here to celebrate it all—mind, body, spirit—and to embrace all that life has to offer, the joy and the pain, and see what the wisdom is in all of it.

In an article you wrote titled "Partying and Skiing," you talk about the reasons why skiers are prone to partying and say, tongue-in-cheek, "Don't worry—scientists have almost separated the skiing and the partying genes in lab rats, and with the use of miniature skis and easy-to-break-out-of-cages, we may have the answers soon." What a hoot! Do you think spirituality can be fun?

Absolutely! The whole question is how spirituality is part of everything. Is it spiritual to be angry? Is it spiritual to be in despair? Is it spiritual to be afraid? Absolutely, yes. Everything can be part of spirituality, if you choose to make it so.

What do you believe about the difference between just going skiing and being in a frame of mind that opens possibilities to deeper knowing?

My favorite quote along those lines is by Helen Keller: "Life is either a daring adventure or nothing at all." So, too, I would say that skiing is either a daring adventure or nothing at all. Skiing is either a place of great wisdom or just not much. The ski industry, of which I was a very integral part for decades, likes to promote itself as a very soulful place—you know, "Mountains are our church." Well, I have to tell you, when I got to the end of my ski career, I wasn't sure that I had learned anything except for the gratification of my own massive ego and a lot of adrenaline! Skiing, unfortunately, gets promoted these days as either a sort of "Hey dude, let's just go and rip it up" or as a family getaway, like a light thing. There's also the question of whether this is an athletic pursuit or a recreational activity. But the reason I started the journey I'm on now is to turn it into something else, to turn it into a spiritual quest or, taking a step back, even a quest just to get to know myself better. I don't think we can learn from experience; I think we learn from *reflecting* on our experience. If people are willing to go on that exploration, if they are ready for that, it can become a deeper journey. I don't believe when we are birthed that we are actually *born*. It is just an invitation to be born. And if we choose to go on that journey, it is there for the taking.

7 *On My Butt Again*

Life Lessons from the Mountain

THOUGHTS FROM KAREN

ADVENTURES IN THE SNOW, by their very nature, have a way of teaching us important spiritual lessons about life. From the "school of hard knocks" to trial-and-error experiments, from the ways we learn to laugh at ourselves to how we engage the learning process to improve our skills, from the ways we push beyond our limits and build confidence to how we analyze risks and sometimes take them—all of these educational experiences are transferable from the mountain into our everyday lives. If you think about it, the entire spiritual journey is really about learning, about being open to whatever God, the Universe, Spirit, Life—however we define our divine teachers—wants to impart to us. If we stop learning, we're not living.

Snow adventures are more than ready to reveal some of these lessons, if we're willing to meet them with a little thoughtful awareness. Here are three lessons in particular that I keep learning, over and over again.

What Goes Up Must Come Down

Sir Isaac Newton went to great pains to create a mathematical equation that spelled out the rules of the law of gravity, and even if we don't understand the math, the bottom line remains the same: what goes up must come down. But what about the inverse? Does what goes down have to come up? In spiritual terms, I think one of the great lessons snow sports can teach us is how to get back up after we've been thrown for a tumble.

Life has a natural cycle of ups and downs, a rhythm of challenges and joyful times, difficulties and celebrations, laughter and tears. The ski mountain offers a poignant metaphor for this reality of life, one we can experience in our bodies as we ascend and descend mountainous terrain. A day on the snow is full of repetitious cycles of climbing up the mountain—whether via a chair lift, climbing skins, cross country skis, or snowshoes—followed by the downward descent provided by gravitational force. This recurring cycle may also include some micropatterns within it, such as sprawling tumbles to the snow and the consequential challenge of struggling to our feet again and again, which are also part of the natural rhythm.

> "Character cannot be developed in ease and quiet. Only through experience of trial and suffering can the soul be strengthened, ambition inspired, and success achieved."
>
> —Helen Keller, deaf-blind author and political activist

At four years old, my son, Zachary, had the opportunity to experience this firsthand. He was having a marvelous time skiing down a long beginner run when a snowboarder, absolutely flying at nearly unimaginable speed, came out of nowhere and plowed into him, sending Zachary flying into the air. He landed on his head and lay there in a small heap. Needless to say, my heart was in my throat as I approached him. The situation appeared disastrous. After crying for a good long while and then discerning that he was not seriously hurt, Zachary, being the trooper that he is, continued skiing. The impact was so intense that he was lucky to escape with only a few scrapes and bruises—and a slightly wounded psyche. To this day, he skis that run looking back behind him to see if anyone is about to crash into him.

Zachary got to learn a powerful lesson that day. Sometimes life can just wallop you from behind and knock you right to the ground. And you won't even see it coming. It can take you by surprise, knock the breath right out of you, and scare you just about to death. So, what do you do? Lie there and writhe and cry and scream? Pitifully take off your equipment and refuse to ski ever again? Look around for someone to blame and keep insisting

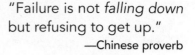

"Failure is not *falling down* but refusing to get up."
—**Chinese** proverb

it's all their fault? No. When the natural rhythm of life wallops you to the ground, it is a chance to learn one of life's great lessons, as my son did: you do what it takes to figure out how to get up. It is my hope that Zachary will carry this learning experience with him throughout his life—and I have the same hope for me, and for you.

Now, I'm not suggesting that getting up is easy. First, you may cry and seek a bit of comfort from loved ones nearby. Tears flow for a host of reasons—pain, overwhelm, shock, fear—but they almost always provide cathartic relief. Expressing emotion can be the necessary transition to defuse the trauma of the event. We should all be so lucky as to have someone come over and pull us into a nurturing embrace when we are knocked down in life. It is one of the tragic illusions of growing up that someone, somewhere, decides we don't need to be cuddled anymore. *Au contraire*. How much kinder and gentler the world would be if we were all ready "comforters" for each other, ready to spring to each other's aid. Perhaps we should all be allowed a five-minute breakdown with tender care each and every day.

Once the initial shock has worn off, you probably take a few deep breaths and do a little check to survey the extent of the damage. For centuries spiritual gurus have extolled the virtues of breathing to reconnect with ourselves and bring ourselves back to the present moment. Breathing has a calming effect and can restore equilibrium. It can bring perspective. Once you're in this more relaxed state, you have the opportunity to account for all your extremities, wiggle your fingers and toes, and make sure your head is still connected. Taking pause is a key response, whether you've been plowed on a ski slope, been in a car accident, gotten fired from a job, or had your heart broken.

> "Success is falling nine times and getting up ten."
> —Jon Bon Jovi, rock singer and actor

Then you begin to tell everyone what happened. This allows you to gather yourself and integrate the event. It takes the "What in the world just happened?" reaction and moves it into your catalog of life experience. The event becomes part of your story. When you tell it as part of your story, hopefully, you will be able to marvel at it in some way.

And then you get back up, dust yourself off, and continue on. This may well be the most important part. It's hardly ever wise to make dramatic declarations—"I'm never playing in the snow again!" or "I'm never getting in a car again!" or "I must be a loser!"—based on one incident. Getting back on the snowboard, or the job search, or the singles network is the only way to keep saying yes to life. The proverbial dusting yourself off is more than the act itself. It is a statement that says, "This is over now, and I am moving on." And you do so, knowing you are stronger than before.

Have you ever struggled through a difficult time and discovered strength, perseverance, and inner resources you didn't know you had?

Backcountry skiers know the challenges of the uphill climb more than most, lungs exploding, legs aching with each upward step. Yet even though the climb can be excruciatingly difficult, a backcountry adventurer wouldn't want to miss a single moment of it. Bill Seline (see the "Conversation with an Adventurer" at the end of chapter 3), backcountry guide and avalanche instructor, describes his experience this way: "It's probably a combination of the endorphins, hard work, nature, micro-route finding skills, and uphill technique that make the climb feel so good and so rewarding. 'Earning your turns,' we backcountry skiers say. For some reason, making turns down a peak after you have climbed it under your own power makes each turn seem more valuable. I am more aware of each turn, its feel, its shape, its fight against gravity."

Just as a backcountry adventurer stands on the precipice looking back at an arduous ascent, often it is only in looking back on a tough time that we can mine its riches. We may be able to feel gratitude for friends found faithful or for a new awareness that we can handle more than we thought we could. Just as the climber gulps in life-giving oxygen, we may feel more alive, more invigorated, and more aware.

Challenging times have a way of stripping away the nonessentials, just as a backcountry climber might make sure his or her pack is as light as possible. This stripping away makes the "up" times more enriching, more joyful. Difficult times can also offer new perspectives, help us tap into our strength, and teach us who we really are. They give us a chance to dig deep spiritually, find our courage, and ask for help.

If All Else Fails ...

... read the instruction manual. This wise, oft-quoted but oft-ignored idiom points to another valuable spiritual learning that plays out in living Technicolor on the mountain: take a lesson. In this case, I'm not talking about what the mountain can teach us, but what we need to be taught before we can approach the mountain. Actually, I'd change the idiom to say, *before* all else fails, go ahead and take a lesson. Just as learning experiences in life sharpen our life skills, so too can lessons for any ability level hone and sharpen skills on the snow.

If you have already signed up for lessons or taken lessons, congratulations; you are among the more evolved of our species! Yet why is it that so many of us are reticent to take lessons? And in life, why is it that we find ourselves "learning" many of the same life lessons over and over again? It seems that certain elements of our personalities, unique to the human species, conspire to create hesitations toward taking lessons. I know many who would rather stay home and bang their thumbs with a hammer. Why is that?

For starters, taking lessons requires that we admit we don't know something. Some of us who drive around, wandering through cities, suburbs, and countrysides, loath to ask for directions. Not being willing to ask for help has some of us staggering under backbreaking loads—literally and metaphorically. Worse, some of us are unwilling to show up at ski school, hard as it is to believe, because we hate being told what to do. We are unwilling to place our bodies at the mercy of someone else's supposed wisdom. Our inner three-year-old wants to rebel and shout, "I can do it myself!" Still, others fear they will look like idiots trying to do what some half-baked instructor thinks is a cute practice drill. If we're going to take risks and be vulnerable, by golly, we'll do it on our own terms!

> "A bend in the road is not the end of the road ... unless you fail to make the turn."
>
> —Anonymous

Taking lessons may well bring us face-to-face with one of the greatest, and hardest, spiritual lessons we need to learn: humility. Approaching a new sport (or taking on any new endeavor) requires that we adopt a measure of humility and let go of our usual ego-driven, image-conscious natures. This gets even harder to do when we consider ourselves "experienced." Much as learning experiences in life are not just for kids, snow sport lessons are not just for novices. Instruction at the intermediate and advanced levels can be priceless for correcting some bad habits, as in, why does my back hurt after I snowboard? Why do I always fall making my left turn on that same steep slope? Why do I seem to catch an edge on the slow, flat areas? A lesson can get you going faster but with more stability and less work. You can be coached in riding untracked or chopped-up powder, tackling the bumps, or mastering terrain park features. You won't believe the improvement a few well-timed tips can make. A professional instructor who knows just how to fine-tune your stance, correct your weight distribution, or enhance how you initiate, move through, and finish your turns can make a huge difference in moving you to your next level of "shredding" or skiing. How much more so can a well-placed spiritual teacher or mentor get us to look at some of our less-than-positive patterns and move us toward more effective ways of operating?

I recently took an advanced snowboarding lesson, my first in many years. After my instructor got me engaged in some simple practice drills to imprint some small adjustments in my brain—I couldn't believe the difference—we headed over to the terrain park. With a few pointers, I slowly, and with great aplomb, landed a few jumps and rode a few "boxes." My instructor was confident I could handle some "rails," but I felt I had accomplished enough for one day.

If by now you have had an attitude adjustment and are signing up for ski lessons, hats off to you! Kudos on making a "turnaround." (When my five-year-old is whining or otherwise needs to change his attitude, we say he needs to have a turnaround. The visual is just as effective for adults.) Now, the question is, where else in life is there need for a turnaround? Where else do egoistic attitudes get in the way of learning and having fun? If you can set aside your need to "know it all" in your winter sports adventures, perhaps you can risk some letting go in other areas. Perhaps you can discard your need to appear all-knowing and take that cooking class you always wanted to take, or that carpentry course, or a hip-hop dancing lesson—even that class on spiritual practice at the church, synagogue, mosque, or retreat center.

People say it takes faith to deepen your spiritual life, but I think it also takes effort: asking questions and reading and learning from people who know more than we do. I value the spiritual guides and teachers I've encountered in my life. Good role models are perhaps the best teachers. I was reminded of this last season when I had an opportunity to ride with the friend of a friend who is an instructor. Because most of my snow adventure buddies are skiers, this was a rare opportunity to board with someone who could push me to the next level.

> "Praise Allah, but first tie your camel to the post."
> —Sufi saying

Although I very much wanted to impress her with my ability, before long I was racing after her, trying to soak up as much of her technique as I could. And I was having a blast! I was aware of how the best teaching happens in its natural arena: I watched, attempted to follow her example, and then experienced it in my own body.

Then I got really brave and asked her to watch me board and offer some pointers. Her suggestions were few, brief, and simple. Again, it reminded me of great spiritual teachings, of profound truths imparted to disciples sitting at the feet of gurus, of advice dispensed in only a few words. It is up to us as students to *live* the wisdom we are taught in order to understand it. The old saying, "When the student is ready, the teacher appears" speaks volumes about how wisdom that is fruitful and timely for our spiritual lives comes to us. The measure of our desire to continue to evolve spiritually is the deciding factor in whether we will participate in the learning opportunities that life offers us.

One of the more recent truths I've learned about taking lessons is that it's never too late to learn. After a few not-that-successful-or-fun attempts at traditional (diagonal stride) cross country skiing, I decided to try it again, but this time with the then relatively new form of the sport called skate skiing (think Olympic biathlon). My young instructor was a jewel, and he encouraged me in some brilliant drills and incremental skill building that had me skate skiing in no time. His passion helped instill in me a great love for the sport that continues to grow. With the basics he taught me, I continue to practice and improve. I can't imagine where I would be without this initial beginning instruction—likely having given up completely on cross country skiing, believing it wasn't for me. Even though I am still fairly new to the sport and skate at a beginner level, I love getting out in the wilderness and savoring a rare precious moment of solitude.

> "Instruction does much, but encouragement does everything."
> —Johann Wolfgang von Goethe, German poet and playwright

I think it is the willingness to learn that helps us really *live* life. Learning calls us to put ourselves on the line and fully engage in the life lessons that present themselves to us. Even when we try something new and are less than successful at first, we learn we can keep trying. We learn that failures and mistakes build character and help us grow spiritual (and intestinal) fortitude more efficiently than anything else. We also learn that we can survive and be better people for it.

What's your relationship with learning? Is it something you eagerly embrace or reluctantly accept? Are there areas in your life where you are particularly unwilling to try a new way of doing something? Where are the old ways broken? Where could you grow by learning a new skill, adopting a new way of communicating, engaging in a new spiritual practice?

If you could drop the mask of being in control and looking cool all the time, you might learn something very valuable. You might find yourself more relaxed and more fun to be with. You might find a joyful new depth to your spiritual self. Discovering that life is a journey and not a destination (not even a ski resort destination) can remind you to relish every moment and embrace all the ongoing lessons that life offers as spiritual learning experiences.

Surviving Those "Was My Face Red!" Moments

The third spiritual life lesson I want to highlight is perhaps best expressed by Elsa Maxwell, gossip columnist and high-society maven in 1930s–1950s Hollywood: "Laugh at yourself first, before anyone else can." As Marcia pointed out in the opening chapter, we don't often think of fun as being spiritual, yet a little play, fun, and humor may be just what we need to lead us to more joy-filled, and even more spiritually aware, existences. Frederic and Mary Ann Brussat, directors of SpiritualityandPractice.com, in *Spiritual Literacy*, express it this way: "Play is a pathway to laughter. All the spiritual traditions have holy fools, clowns, or tricksters who try to tease people into a fuller appreciation of the paradox and mystery of life.... Playing around is a good and holy thing. Don't ever let anyone tell you otherwise."

> "Nature has no mercy at all. Nature says, 'I'm going to snow. If you have on a bikini and no snowshoes, that's tough. I am going to snow anyway.'"
> —Maya Angelou, American poet

Many of us spend too much time being hard on ourselves. Sometimes we engage way too much of our time and energy in the "image management" business, trying to appear a certain way at all times. How exhausting. Snow adventuring provides some wonderful opportunities to bust us out of the carefully controlled images we try to exude of ourselves as graceful, intelligent, competent, agile, and in control. A few choice, less-than-perfect experiences on snow can be great practice for the taking-ourselves-too-seriously antidote: casting our carefully controlled images to the wind and erupting in a long, loud, healing belly laugh. It is good for the soul to look ridiculous once in a while. We are, after all, human and ingeniously *not* made to be robots. What a great lesson to figure out how to laugh at ourselves, however awkward we may appear.

I am a people-watcher. Sometimes I see people who interest me for some reason, and I find myself thinking, "I wonder what their life is like. What is their story?" I especially do this when I see something that catches my attention, like individuals wearing goofy hats at ski resorts. I wonder what lives in them that is so giddy, so joyful, so confident that they can gift the rest of us with a smile when we see them. I think of the time when

> "Sometimes the littlest things in life are the hardest to take. You can sit on a mountain more comfortably than on a tack."
> —Anonymous

my family and I, after attending an Easter sunrise service, donned our helmets, which we had adorned the night before with large pink and white bunny ears, and had a blast skiing and riding all afternoon, relishing the grins that came our way.

The calamitously hysterical and humblingly helpless opportunities for laughing at ourselves in snow come in an unlimited variety of forms. Nothing can take an embarrassing moment on skis or a board and turn it into hilarious adventure quite like a Warren Miller ski movie. I remember a scene of people and skis coming off the lift in a tangled heap, with more folks landing on the pile two by two. "Lifties"—in fast motion reminiscent of Charlie Chaplin slapstick—stomping on bindings, popping skis off, and tossing them into another growing pile a few feet away. Side splitting.

And then there are the irresistible laughs that snow tumbles invite. On many occasions, I have witnessed folks falling over while standing still. This is perhaps best accomplished when it happens in the lift line in front of many people who look sharply down at you, as if to say, "What are you doing down there, and why are you slowing the line down?"

Or picture this: you are on the long approach, returning to the cross country center through a meadow that is in full view of everyone inside and out, especially those eating, drinking, and relaxing on the deck. (Cross country skiers tend to take their sport somewhat seriously. You just don't see the element of goofiness at cross country centers that you do at ski resorts.) You make your graceful approach, and just as you are thinking, "Okay, lookin' cool," as if you know what you're doing, something unexpected happens. Skis and poles get all tangled up, and you go flying—arms, legs, poles, and skis flailing in chaotic jerks. You finally, somehow, recover just in time to see faces on the deck hide their smirks, pretending that the food is suddenly very interesting.

"Every survival kit should include a sense of humor."
—Anonymous

Or take the skier or boarder who is unable to stop as planned and skids right into the crowd-control liftie. I have seen advanced skiers and riders find themselves in straddle position when they get a ski or board stuck on the wrong side of the lift lane pole. They then must back up—where folks have already crowded in behind—in order to proceed. I have seen parents, while attempting to teach their little angels to ski, execute an impressive slow-motion fall, grasping at anything and everything on the way down, finally taking their kids down with them. And I have been every one of these.

Anne Lamott (see the "Conversation with an Adventurer" at the end of chapter 1) describes an experience familiar to many of us in *Grace (Eventually): Thoughts on Faith*:

> Not too long ago, I was skiing in the mountains where my son, Sam, and I spend a weekend most winters. Nowadays, he instantly disappears with the hordes of snowboarders. I believe he is somewhat embarrassed to be seen with me: once, standing next to him and his friend at the bottom of a hill, I fell over for no reason. And in fact, the very first time we went skiing together, I skied in a strange, slow, inexorable path for a hundred feet or so, straight into a huge net at the bottom of the slopes, erected to protect the small Ski Bear children from being crushed. Then I got tangled up in it, like a fish.

Recognize yourself in any of these situations? Even the most skilled and proficient skiers/boarders have experienced a few moments of looking exceedingly clumsy and incompetent on the snow. Need a moment of comic relief? Just stand and people-watch for a while. You'll probably be grinning in no time. These comedic moments happen to all of us, even though they may be far from our usually smooth MO. Then again, you really should-n't laugh *too* much (unless it's your ski buddy—then go ahead, laugh your patooti off) because, in the blink of an eye, it might be you. Strapping one or two sticks on your feet and trying to get around on a slippery surface is a great equalizer, and the one flailing and looking ridiculous could be any one of us. Taking ourselves lightly and taking things in stride as part of life are a great way to remain relatively drama free and a wonderful tool for recovering from a host of unexpected experiences in life.

Keeping our sense of humor honed and active may be the best gift we can give ourselves, and it surely is a gift from the Divine. I have no doubt that God has a keen sense of humor, even a goofy, playful jokester side. In her book *Laughing Your Way to Grace* (SkyLight Paths), Susan Sparks—a trial lawyer turned minister, turned stand-up comedian—calls laughter a "GPS system for the soul." She imagines what God might have to say to us about our lack of laughter: "Where's your sense of humor? Did someone steal it? Did you lose it? Is it in the same place as those missing keys and umbrellas? I mean, come on! I gave you laughter as your first gift. A baby gift—don't you remember? Well, the sad truth is, unless you are under twelve years old or over seventy, you may *not*.... But it's in those in-between years—those years when you think you are the sole proprietor of the universe—that you need this gift the most."

> "A person without a sense of humor is like a wagon without springs—jolted by every pebble in the road."
> —Henry Ward Beecher, nineteenth-century clergyman, reformer, and abolitionist

As Susan says, "For those who think God doesn't laugh, think platypus and blowfish." Knowing that the Creator of all things funny laughs with us in unconditional love goes a long way toward encouraging us to laugh at ourselves. So go ahead, keep it fun. Don't take yourself too seriously. How could you possibly? You just strapped a stick or two onto your feet to be launched downhill and allow gravity to have its way with you.

Take some advice from a conversation I heard recently in a lift line, with applications way beyond the ski hill. Patient and wise dad to whining daughter: "You can have fun. Or not. It's your choice." Wise counsel, not just for being on the mountain but for the unabridged version of the spiritual journey that is life.

I am moved by champion snowboarder Evan Strong's statement, "If you can't laugh about life, why are you living?" You can read more of his story in the "Conversation with an Adventurer" at the end of this chapter, but I want to share this one vignette where he describes his sense of humor:

> Six or seven months after I lost my leg, I got my prosthesis. That was way too premature and I did damage. I just wanted to walk. As soon as I got out of the hospital, I wanted to ride my skateboard. I would stand on it and use my crutches to push myself up and down my neighborhood just to be on my board. I had a standard-shift truck, and I would drive it around with my crutch, using it like my left leg to push in the clutch. I got pulled over by a cop, and just to be a rascal, I asked, "Is this illegal?" He did not know what to say. He didn't want to give me a hard time 'cause I had one leg. So he was like, "I really don't know if that's illegal," and he let me go.
>
> I wanted to live my life 'cause I still had it. I would make up funny stories if somebody asked, just to shock them. I had a good sense of humor, I still do. If you can't laugh about life, why are you living?

Once you've given yourself permission to align with the most goofy and unselfconscious free spirits on the mountain, you might feel as if you can fly, so surprisingly unfettered are you. The important learning happens when you can transfer this to your daily life. What are the elements of everyday living that you take all too seriously? Where do you work so hard that your creativity is choked right out of you? What if you took yourself a little less seriously? What would happen if you wore a silly hat to pick up your kids from school? What if you listened to comedy on the way to work instead of the news? What if you decided that it took way too much energy to be self-conscious? What if you stopped hypercontrolling the images you project to the world?

❊ A Reflective Moment

When you bring more humor, play, levity, and lightness into your spiritual life, it will spill over into every area of your life, because really there is no separation. It is in that spirit, with great respect and humble deference to the twelve-step program of Alcoholics Anonymous, that I offer the "Twelve Steps of Getting Over Yourself" in order to become a certified snow adventurer:

1) We admitted we were powerless over the snowy mountain, that our lives were in danger.
2) We came to believe that a Power greater than ourselves could get us down the mountain.
3) We made a decision to turn our will and our lives over to the care of a wise and patient ski or snowboard instructor.
4) We made a searching and tireless inventory of our fears.
5) We admitted to God, to ourselves, and to another human being the exact nature of our clumsiness.
6) We were entirely ready to have God remove all these obstacles to our getting down the mountain before lunch.
7) We humbly asked God to carefully remove our fogged-up goggles and our reluctance to ask for help in the form of lessons.
8) We made a list of all persons we almost ran into, and did run into, and became willing to make amends to them all.
9) We made direct amends to such people whenever possible, except when to do so would surely make them fall down.
10) We continued to take personal inventory, and when we were careening out of control, we promptly admitted it.
11) We sought through prayer and meditation to improve our conscious contact with the mountain, praying only

for our instructor's will for us and the power to carry that out.

12) Having had a spiritual awakening as a result of these steps, we tried to carry this message to others lying about and flailing on beginner slopes, and to practice these principles in all our affairs.

Conversation with an Adventurer
Evan Strong, adaptive snowboarder

~

Evan Strong, at twenty-two, is a two-time national superpipe champion and gold medalist in slope style in the Adaptive Division of the USASA (United States of America Snowboard Association). He is working to get snowboarding competitions sanctioned as official events of the Paralympics. A raw food chef and restaurant owner, he whimsically refers to himself as a "monopod."

How is snowboarding a spiritual experience for you?

The absolute quietness of being in trees in a storm on a powder day … it is so peaceful and so quiet, but it can be so violent and stormy. It is awe inspiring, seeing white all around and having nobody else around. I see God in those moments. Like, how could God *not* be here right now? I just see God playing in the trees, in the wind, in the snow, so in those moments, I am able to just see through the veil a bit more. When I'm in the snow and nature, when divine consciousness is just doing its own thing, I'm able to witness that and to dance with it down a mountain. Does it get any better than that? I want my whole life to be experiencing that magic—can I even call it magic? On my snowboard I want to experience that part of nature that is perfection within itself.

You've been through quite a life-changing experience …

The accident was ten days before my eighteenth birthday. Before I lost my leg, I thought I was invincible … like, I can't break. With that mentality, a motorcycle totally fit me. I rode it six months, no problems, and this one day coming home from work, I was just following behind a car in front of me, and I noticed on the inside lane a white SUV coming at me, and BOOM! I have a conscious memory of hitting my head on the car, and the next moment I was looking up at the sky, with a guardrail on my left. I looked down over myself, and my jeans were literally blown off of me, and my thigh was smashed wide open, laid over my chest. At that point the pain really began to set in, and it was so intense I almost couldn't stand being in my own skin anymore.

I've been meditating since I was four and have been practicing yoga since I was very young. We are given a mantra in meditation to help calm the mind so spirit can emerge, so I started repeating this mantra I've known since I was little. At that moment, all pain subsided. My guru who taught me my meditation actually came to me, and in that moment I asked my guru, "Am I going to die?" Then I had a sense of knowing, "No, you still have work to do here." A couple minutes later, a lady who had just done her laundry and was driving back to her house saw me, and she packed my wounds with her laundry so I didn't bleed to death right there.

Then what happened?

I was four weeks in the hospital, five surgeries, and one week in ICU. By the end of it, I knew that people had prosthetic legs and could do amazing things, but I really didn't know how it worked. But I thought, "If they can do it, I can do it. I know where I want to be, and I have the willpower. I don't know how it's gonna happen, or how long it's gonna take, but I'm here for the fight."

I started like an infant. I needed everyone to do everything for me. Slowly, slowly, I rebuilt my life again. In one sense, I did die on the side of the road … the Evan that I was is not the Evan who is here now.

What are some of the life lessons that experience taught you?

A very huge life lesson. When I was younger, I was really impatient, I wanted my gratification now, constantly … I know what I want, and I want it *now*. But life doesn't work that way. I was forced to learn patience. In order to get the results I wanted, I had to be patient. I'm still trying to master that, but I'm a lot better now than I was. Now I know that there is divine timing for everything.

Another huge lesson is compassion. When you have compassion for all living things, then all living things have compassion for you. That is an extremely profound experience. Love and you will be loved.

Another really amazing life lesson I learned is that I am not invincible. That came as quite a shock. I still feel pretty invincible, but now I know I have limitations.

How has it changed the course of your life?

I believe we are beings of joy; I don't believe we are meant to suffer. Losing my leg is the worst thing that ever happened to me, but it is also the best thing that ever happened to me. So many great things have happened. If I didn't lose my leg, would I get to go snowboarding and see all these wonderful places and get to meet so many amazing people who had similar experiences, and to get to work with them? That's priceless. Going to the Olympics, going to the X-Games, going to nationals ... I could spend my whole life training to try and make that happen, and it might not ever happen. My greatest dreams are coming true because of my accident. I'm so blessed.

You mentioned differences between the old Evan and the postaccident Evan ...

The world looks completely different. It's fuller ... there's more color ... there's more beauty ... there's more things to smile about ... food tastes better now ... tea is sweeter ... friendships are more amazing and I cherish them more ... music is moving ... colors are delicious. Through that experience, I am grateful for everything, and everything is grateful for me. When you put that kind of energy out, it comes right back to you. It's a hobby of mine, especially when I travel, to talk to a stranger and see his or her point of view on things. It's profound. It's an appreciation that I don't think I had much at all when I was younger, as a punky skater kid.

I want to experience new things now, now that I have the perspective that my life has been given back to me. My next thing is I'm going to learn how to white-water kayak. I'm doing my first white-water clinic this month just because it is going to be one more way to experience God. I'm alive, so let's live it!

Tell me about learning to snowboard.

After recovering, getting my prosthesis, and starting to get my mobility back, I thought, "Okay, I've never tried snowboarding before; let's make it happen. My will was so strong. My uncle—he is one of my heroes—brought me out to Sun Valley, Idaho. We went mountain biking a lot before and after losing my leg. He believed me when I said I could do these things, and said, "Great, let's go do it!" Before I went up on the lift, I hiked myself up little hills, stood up and tried to turn—and fell on my butt. Eventually, I was connecting turns on my own. Having a skateboarding background, I found it very similar. By the end of the day, I was going down every run in that small resort. The next day I was doing black diamonds.

Anything you want people to know?

Actually, being disabled is a state of mind. You learn something new every day. Experience a different taste, if that is your thing. Try something new, live your life differently. You don't need to go through what I went through to see the simple beauty in life. I want people to get off their butts, get off the couch, turn off the TV, and go snowboarding. Go experience God in those peaceful moments, because everybody can. People limit themselves, people don't believe in themselves. There is a saying, "If you believe you can do something, or if you believe you can't do something, either way, you are right!" So I want people to know that anything is possible. Go experience beauty. I do, and it's the best thing ever. I try and lift people up that way. There's one message I really want to get across in my mentorship with nonprofit organizations: "Love your life, enjoy your life, be grateful for your life, show it through actions every day by how you live your life. Learn to experience and see the beauty all around you. Being in the snow is a great way to do it. Find your joy. Live your joy. Be your joy." That would be my message.

Making a Difference

8

Putting Spirituality into Action for the Planet and Its Peoples

THOUGHTS FROM KAREN

THROUGHOUT THIS BOOK we have offered some alternative ways of looking at and engaging in spiritual practice: reflecting with our minds and hearts out on the mountain, meditating with our bodies hiking in the woods, praying with our hands touching and savoring snowflakes. We are limited only by our creativity of how we might put our spirituality into action. Yet a spirituality that has only an inward focus, however comforting it may feel initially, winds up being self-serving and self-absorbed, and therefore misses the point entirely.

The story is told of a man who appeared before God, his heart breaking from the sorrow and injustice in the world, who cried out, "God, look at all the suffering everywhere, the pain and anguish in your world. Why don't you send help?"

And God replied, "I did send help. I sent you."

A jarring message to be sure, and that is a good thing if, in fact, it gets our attention and moves us out of our complacency. Virtually all great spiritual teachers have taught in some way that we are called to make a difference: to feed the hungry, provide for the poor, help those less fortunate. At first glance, it may be hard to imagine how this might apply to snow sports. Obviously, there are plenty of comfortable folks around ski slopes, since, because of the costs involved, it is principally a sport for the economically comfortable, if not privileged. Yet because of this, the slopes are an opportune place to capitalize on the critical mass of those who have the resources to make a difference.

To many, the snow sports industry may appear to be about only making money. It might surprise you to learn of many worthwhile humanitarian involvements and causes that have their roots in the industry. This is why I feel it is so important to share these endeavors that have a higher purpose. While the folks involved in these efforts may or may not have given thought to spirituality or experienced it as a motivating force, they certainly seem to understand some of the reasons we are here on this earth: to make the world a better place, ensuring that we leave it better than we found it, and to alleviate suffering where we encounter it, bringing a measure of joy where we can.

> "Don't ask yourself what the world needs. Ask yourself what makes you come alive and then go do that. Because what the world needs is people who have come alive."
>
> —Dr. Howard Thurman, civil rights leader, author, theologian, and educator

Trying to make a difference is not about making ourselves feel good and righteous, although feelings of satisfaction and fulfillment often do occur. Rather, the effort emanates from understanding our oneness with all who share this planet (and with the planet itself!). It evolves out of our gratitude for this precious life and the realization that most of us have more resources than we really need.

In these mountain cathedrals of profound beauty where we connect with our passions, we can also connect with our best and higher selves, and with something larger than ourselves. This helps us better understand our place in the world. It is out of this understanding and the gratitude we experience that the desire arises to be about something more than "just us."

Making a Difference on the Mountain

One of the important areas where snow sports are having a powerful impact is in the area of adaptive programs for people with disabilities. Many mountain resort areas all over the world have adaptive ski, cross country, and snowboard programs that allow differently abled persons to experience the thrills and spiritual adventures of snow sports. Specialized equipment and instruction facilitate this exciting opportunity, thanks to the early efforts of a group of World War II veterans who developed techniques and equipment that enabled single-leg amputees to ski.

In later years, adaptive ski technology and instructional programs advanced as vets from the Tenth Mountain Division began teaching disabled Vietnam vets how to ski, and the first disabled skiing organization was born. The Far West chapter, operating out of Alpine Meadows Resort in the Lake Tahoe area, is the founding chapter of Disabled Sports USA, which is the nation's largest non-profit multi-sport and multidisability organization. Today there are more than ninety chapters serving more than sixty thousand people nationwide.

> "For people who have been told they can't participate in this kind of recreation, to be able to share it with their family and friends, it's the best thing going."
>
> —Alpine Meadows, adaptive ski instructor for over thirty years

The Alpine Meadows program has more than two hundred volunteers, who give thousands of hours each year so that many adaptive skiers and snowboarders can participate in snow sports. Participants embrace the program's motto, "If I can do this, I can do anything," which exemplifies the program's mission of providing affordable and inclusive sports and recreation for people with disabilities so they can build health and confidence.

Skiing and other fun and challenging activities are an important part of the rehabilitation of injured military personnel. In an article that appeared in the *Sierra Sun*, staff writer Nick Cruit described the Wounded Warriors Project, which, in conjunction with Disabled Sports USA, recently enabled sixteen veterans to learn how to ski and snowboard at Alpine Meadows. At first, many are hesitant and are not sure they can do it, but by the end of the day, it is difficult to get them off the mountain. Private Drew Goin, who lost his left eye and suffers from a brain injury, had difficulty with balance initially but was flying off jumps and throwing 180-degree turns in the air by day's end. Andrew Bradley, who lost his right leg to a roadside bomb in Iraq, had never really even seen snow. He considered skiing on one leg no greater challenge than that posed by gravity and the slippery surface.

Other disabled veterans are finding equally rewarding ways to experience the mountain. When Tony Steiner, who served as a medic in the Pacific from 1943 to 1946, learned that he had macular degeneration and had to have one eye lasered about eight years ago, he was devastated.

But as I watched other veterans at the Reno VA Hospital, I felt I had some plus marks going for me. One of the reasons we live at Tahoe is our joy of skiing. As my eyesight deteriorated, I had to adjust my ski days. If it is overcast (flat light), I stay at home. But on a sunny day … AH! That's the time to challenge the gods! I ski a bit slower now. At eighty-four my body is more fragile, and if I fall, it is not so easy to get up.

My greatest joy recently was to join the American Disabled Veterans at Snowmass, Colorado. I was among five hundred disabled veterans. My guide for blind skiers took me all the way to the top at 11,800 feet on Big Burn, and I skied behind her. That was a thrill and my most spiritual moment in my life. If I am around next year, I hope to return—challenge myself and get the Rocky Mountain high. That would be a heavenly feeling and very exuberant.

What could be a more spiritual endeavor for people than to feel the sun and the wind on their beaming faces, while gliding down a tree-lined slope and feeling their body in joyous exuberance, exclaiming, "I *can!*"; to be able to celebrate an accomplishment of something they never thought possible? What could be more spiritual than to be the one to assist in making this feat happen, finding that joy and exuberance are overwhelmingly contagious?

Making a Difference in Community

In my community of Truckee, Northstar Resort hosts "Noel Nights" during the holidays, complete with Santa and carolers. Bringing a can of food for the local food bank, Project Manna, earns participants free ice-skate rentals. Part of the annual tradition is a contest between employees on the mountain and those in the village, aimed at which area of the resort can collect the largest contribution on behalf of Truckee Community Christmas. This past season, employees donated barrels of canned food and more than $1,600 in cash to this local project that helps hundreds of families and seniors at holiday time with food, toys, gifts, warm coats, and food gift cards.

Northstar also hosted Tahoe Women's Services Ski Day, and nearly one thousand skiers and snowboarders came out to support this local nonprofit, which provides emergency food and shelter, counseling, legal assistance, and advocacy to women and families in need. Full-day adult lift tickets were sold at a discounted price, resulting in a total of $25,000 raised for the organization.

Together with its sister resort, Sierra-at-Tahoe, Northstar donated close to $250,000 during the 2008–2009 winter season alone to support local students and athletes, and environmental and community organizations. "Part of our role as members of the Tahoe business community and as global citizens is finding ways to give back throughout the season," commented John Rice, general manager of Sierra-at-Tahoe Resort.

Both resorts also participate in the Skiing for Schools program, with each resort sponsoring a weekend day during the season to support education. Lift tickets are offered at a drastic discount, and proceeds go to local schools.

Maybe I'm "bragging" a little about my local community, but my point is that this kind of thing is going on all over the world, at all kinds of mountain resorts. Next time you're at your favorite ski area, check out what they are doing to make a difference in their community. You might even want to join in their efforts.

Ski area foundations, like many community foundations, are uniquely and ideally positioned to raise significant funds for community organizations that provide direct services to local residents. For example, Wild Wings Cross Country Center in Peru, Vermont, hosts a Ski for Heat fund-raiser each winter that helps low-income families and individuals with their heating bills. More than $125,000 has been raised for heating fuel assistance since the event started in 2001.

Soul of the Summit, the Summit Foundation of Summit County, Colorado, has, since 1986, awarded more than $8.6 million in grants that have been distributed to 265 nonprofit organizations. These organizations improve the quality of life in each community by fostering art and culture, health and human services, education, environmental projects, and sports and recre-

> "Helping out is not some special skill. It is not the domain of rare individuals. It is not confined to a single part or time of our lives. We simply heed the call of that natural caring impulse and follow where it leads."
>
> —Ram Dass, *How Can I Help?*

ational activities. In addition, the foundation has awarded more than $1 million to students pursuing postsecondary education.

The Summit Foundation prides itself on being a community leader in the building of a "legacy of generosity." Formerly operated by the Breckenridge Ski Corporation, the Summit Foundation is now a partnership of many of the area ski resorts, including Arapahoe Basin, Beaver Creek, Breckenridge, Copper Mountain, Keystone, Vail, and Winter Park. The foundation's goal is to "assist those in need with a 'hand up' rather than a 'hand out.'" The foundation raises in excess of $1.3 million each year through donations, fund-raising, charitable and memorial gifts, and its signa-

> "God has no hands or feet or voice except ours and through these [God] works."
> —Teresa of Avila, sixteenth-century mystic

ture multiresort "donor pass" programs. Donor passes are offered at two different donation levels; one is good at five resorts, the other at all seven. The pass holder is rewarded with discounts on goods and services at each resort, and proceeds from the passes go directly into the community to support non-profit organizations.

Similarly, the Whistler Blackcomb Foundation was formed in 1992 to strengthen the role of the Whistler Blackcomb resort as a supporter of the community. Since then, it has raised more than $4.2 million for nonprofit programs in the "sea to sky corridor" of British Columbia, Canada. It funds programs with emphasis on children, youth, and family programs. The signature event of the Whistler Blackcomb Foundation is its TELUS Winter Classic, a full weekend of events featuring wine and cheese tastings, ski races, and a mountaintop gala, dance, and auction that hosts more than eight hundred guests.

We all emanate from the same Source, and if we allow our illusions of separateness to fall away, it is a profound realization to look around and experience the world as one community. How might we live out this realization in our lives? I can think of two people in particular who have put their vibrant passion into action and ignited a change in the world beyond their own local communities.

Hannah Teeter scored Olympic gold in 2006 in snowboarding halfpipe in Torino, Italy. She also spun into gold her childhood hobby of helping her dad collect and make maple syrup by creating a nonprofit venture called Hannah's Gold. All the proceeds of this organization help the people of Kirondon, Kenya, improve their quality of life. Hannah's Gold has built an addition on an overcrowded school and helped fund water sanitation projects at four other schools, where the kids were previously drinking disease-infested water. When Hannah attended the opening ceremony for the school addition, she was astounded to be greeted by seven hundred kids, who presented gifts of handmade jewelry and shawls and performed songs and dances.

> "The question of bread for myself is a material question, but the question of bread for my neighbor is a spiritual question."
>
> —Nikolai Berdyaev, religious and political philosopher

"I cannot express how thankful these community members and children were to have clean water," exclaims Hannah. She encourages all of us to get involved: "We can help, we already have and will continue to do so. Let's do this!"

Warren Miller, pioneer of ski action films, codeveloped the Warren Miller Freedom Foundation with his wife, Laurie. The purpose of the foundation is to teach young folks how to develop, market, and run a business—and more important, as their mission statement affirms, "to leave the program with confidence, information, and life-skills that inspire future creativity and business ventures." To date, nearly sixteen hundred people have gone through the ten-week program, and they are now adding a program for adults.

These are just a few examples of how people in the snow sports community are making a difference. Marcia and I would like to support the effort of people changing our world for the better, so if you know of other people within the snow sports industry who are working to make a difference, let us know. We'd like to feature them on our website, www.spiritualadventuresinthesnow.com. We'd also like to invite you to reflect on the possibilities for ways you might get involved. How might you use your passion for snow sports to make a difference?

❄ A *Reflective Moment*

Sit for a few moments with a sense of profound gratitude. Just as your passion gets ignited in the snow, allow your passion to be ignited by imagining how you could make a difference. Here are a few ideas to jump-start your thinking:

- *Volunteer.* Adaptive ski programs are extremely rewarding programs and are always looking for volunteers. Consider taking your group on a different kind of ski trip: volunteer with an adaptive program in the morning, and ski in the afternoon. Or volunteer with a Boarding for Breast Cancer event. Or take an afternoon during the ski trip to volunteer at a local service organization. Not only will you make a difference in people's lives, but it is also a great opportunity to get to know the local community beyond the resort. And don't forget "voluntourism." If voluntourism is the fastest growing segment of the travel industry, why should travel to snowy mountain vistas be left out? Ski voluntourism or snow voluntourism is poised to capitalize on the trend and is only limited by your imagination. What might it look like for you?

- *Initiate a group service project.* If your family vacations with other families, plan a vacation together that includes a service project. Or host an organizational meeting and do a service project together. Or get your local ski club to do a project or collect food for the local food bank. Some easy service projects include the following:
  - Provide backpacks with school supplies for a local Head Start preschool. (This will take a little research and coordination. Local family resource centers can direct you to where the needs are.)
  - Make baby kits or school bags to be distributed by service organizations during times of national disasters.
- *Build community on the mountain.* On the mountain, many of us experience a more than superficial connection with those who share our passion for snow sports. Our desire to make these connections is different than "meeting people," because the effort springs from the understanding that we are already kindred spirits. Here are some ideas for intentionally building community:
  - Check on fallen skiers/riders to make sure they are not hurt, and if they are, alert ski patrol.
  - Collect items from their "yard sale" (the results of a spectacular fall—see p. 186), especially if, as is usually the case, they are downhill from their stuff. When folks observe people helping people, the resulting "warm fuzzies" are contagious, and they will be more likely to do the same.
  - Be friendly and courteous in lift lines and on lifts. If you're a skier, be a "pole pal" (see p. 183) to a snowboarder stuck on the flats.

It doesn't have to be all about you. Together, we can change the world … a little at a time.

Making a Difference on Behalf of the Planet

As the French philosopher and mystic Teilhard de Chardin said, "We are not human beings having a spiritual experience, we are spiritual beings having a human experience." If we subscribe to this idea that we are something more than the atoms that hold together our bones and flesh, something more than the physical matter that forms our bodies, then what are we exactly? What is this part of us that has been called soul or spirit? What is it in us that wants to create a higher good, that feels a kinship with all beings? What is the desire that causes us to seek a connection with something larger than ourselves? Many would call it a spark of Divine Presence that lives in us. Some would say that we are created in the image of God and are therefore innately connected to the Creator. Whatever language you use to describe this spiritual connection, how does it translate to your relationship to the earth and its other inhabitants?

Some folks feel that it is our human right to use every resource and animal on the earth. After all, the earth was given to humankind by God, right? On the other hand, some folks feel that we should spend large sums of money saving every animal and plant species,

> "I don't know what your destiny will be, but one thing I do know: the only ones among you who will be really happy are those who have sought and found how to serve."
>
> —Albert Schweitzer, physician, philosopher, and theologian

no matter how minute, that has ever lived on the earth. And there is every response in between. No matter where you stand on this spectrum, perhaps as spiritual beings we can agree that we have been given the care of the earth, and the ground on which we stand is holy ground. How can we look deep into our souls and not want to reverse the damage that humankind has done to the planet?

Imagine this scene. *Place*: ski town anywhere on planet earth. *Time*: mid-December, any year in the 2000s. The town is awash in twinkly lights dancing in trees; large candy canes with red ribbons adorn the street lights. But the conversations among those out and about are not about the upcoming holiday. They are talking in hushed tones, searching each other's faces for signs of hope. "Think we'll get some snow this weekend?" "When do you think we'll see a storm?" If anyone mentions they saw a hint of snow in the forecast, all eyes and ears turn in their direction. "Calling for snow *when*?" "You heard it *where*? "How much?" No one dares say out loud the unspeakable that is on everyone's mind: Will this be the year we are drastically affected by climate change? Will this be the one known as the winter that wasn't?

> "The migration of fauna and flora up the mountains to cooler climates has already begun. Not surprisingly, the snowpack is moving along with the climate."
>
> —forceChange.com

Ski resorts, and the ski resort towns that have developed around them, stand to be drastically affected by the devastating fallout of global warming. It's not just that the locals love the white stuff and would miss their snow adventuring; economies of entire mountain regions rely on the influx of winter enthusiasts and the seasonal resort workforce. The anxiety mounts proportionately as more and more snowless December days are marked off on the calendar. Few occurrences are more discouraging than to have substantial snow in the forecast only to have the storm arrive and deliver nothing measurable or, worse, rain. Nothing is gloomier than a weeklong rainstorm in the midst of an already disheartening winter. Locals who live in these resort towns know firsthand what a difference just a few feet of altitude within microclimates can make in weather patterns. One neighborhood might receive a couple of feet of snow; another a mile away might receive twice as much. The elementary school might receive a few inches of snow; the downtown area might receive rain. As rising temperatures cause the altitude levels of snowfall to rise, the results could be catastrophic for ski areas and their regional economies.

Given the severe outlook of this situation with its potential consequences, you might think that ski resorts and their surrounding towns would be on the cutting edge of diligent attempts to reverse climate change, but surprisingly, this is not always the case. American author Barbara Kingsolver offers a fitting dose of reality in *Animal, Vegetable, Miracle*: "Believing in the righteousness of a piece of work, alas, is not what gets it done." Many resorts, however, are hard at work increasing their efforts to reduce their carbon footprint and are making progress in numerous areas.

Perhaps the most controversial area, and where resorts get very mixed reviews, depending on whom you talk to, is in the area of environmental protection. Resort managers and owners feel they need to develop and expand to compete for tourist visits and dollars. Development and expansion means more than just cutting down copious amounts of trees, which is devastating enough; it also means disturbing ecosystems, destroying some of the natural habitat of wildlife, and rerouting natural flows of water, which alters more ecosystems. Some resorts are now beginning to pay attention to public

"Likely major effects [of global warming] on the ... ski industry would include a shorter ski season and increased reliance on artificial snowmaking. The season would be squeezed at both ends, fall and spring, and attempts to make up for a natural-snow deficit with man-made snow could backfire due to warmer temperatures."

—Jim Erickson, *Rocky Mountain News*

outcry—and the demands of often rigorous requirements of town governments—to expand and develop responsibly, with an eye toward the long-term preservation of this precious God-given natural resource, our mountain wilderness.

Ski areas are also seeking alternative energy sources to fuel their operations. Harnessing wind energy and pholtaic solar cell energy to power buildings and ski lifts, and utilizing biofuels and electric engines to fuel resort transportation vehicles, are becoming more commonplace. These alternative energy sources boast the added benefit that they burn cleaner and pollute the environment with less toxic emissions. How many of us have enjoyed a beautiful day on the slopes, breathing pristine mountain air, only to find ourselves at day's end in a cloud of black smoke belched out by a resort bus? Hopefully, these experiences are becoming a thing of the past.

When I choose to spend my hard-earned dollars at a resort, I want to know that my resort of choice is taking great pains to take care of Mother Earth. I am unhappy when I must throw my plastic plate from my burrito and the cardboard from my riding buddy's burger and our drink cups into the trash simply because I cannot find a recycling receptacle. It overjoys me to visit a resort where I never encounter a trash bin without seeing a recycling bin next to it. These resorts get even higher marks when the same situation exists not only in the village at base level but also high on the mountain. Additionally, I'd like to see resort lodging units provide guests

"In the U.S., 4.39 pounds of trash per day and up to 56 tons of trash per year are created by the average person. Every year we fill enough garbage trucks to form a line that would stretch from the earth, half-way to the moon. Each day the U.S. throws away enough trash to fill 63,000 garbage trucks. Almost ⅓ of the waste generated is packaging."
—Clean Air Council

with easy-to-understand instructions (in multiple languages) for sorting recyclable waste. The resorts whose best practices include diligent recycling deserve lots of credit for their efforts. Wouldn't it be wonderful if every resort venue were doing this?

Unfortunately, the travel and leisure industry does not have a reputation (yet!) of taking great pains to recycle its refuse and reduce its inordinate amount of waste. If ski resorts and other recreational venues—stadiums, amusement parks, hotels, cruise ships, movie theaters—took a serious look at the packaging of the retail products that they are distributing and made recycling receptacles very available, think of the waste that could be drastically reduced.

Many resorts are getting quite creative in their efforts to mitigate climate change and "go green." Sugar Bowl, in northern California, hosts an Environmental Awareness Day for the purpose of education, inviting attendees to take part in the ski area's green efforts. Guests participate in green art projects and informational activities, while the resort solicits public commitment to reduce greenhouse gases with practical measures.

Whistler Blackcomb in Vancouver has inaugurated an environmental team as part of their management staff. Having reduced waste over the past few years by 59 percent, the team is charged with working toward such goals as zero waste output, internal and external sustainability training, energy conservation, hazardous materials management, climate change mitigation, and community outreach.

Aspen/Snowmass in Colorado, regarded as the center of the green ski movement, has produced a collaborative community campaign complete with television advertising and a comprehensive website, www.savesnow.org. The site contains a plethora of information detailing sustainable efforts at the resort and provides education about the climate change crisis. The site encourages people to get involved in the Save Snow effort with commitments that go beyond the usual practical ideas.

Park City, Utah, running on 100 percent renewable energy, has decreased its snowmobile fleet by 30 percent to reduce carbon dioxide emissions, is fueling its entire snowcat fleet with biodiesel, and prints its mountain guides on recycled paper. Copper Mountain, Colorado, is now 100 percent wind-powered and rewards carpoolers on several Saturdays during the season by offering preferred parking and lunch discounts. Alpine Meadows, in the Lake Tahoe area of northern California, has a Rideshare Board on its website where you can "search and post rides to your favorite resort, hook up carpools, save money and gas, make new friends, and have a lot of fun doing it." In addition to being 100 percent powered by renewable energy and fueling its shuttle fleet with biodiesel, Mt. Bachelor in Oregon has instituted a "No Idling" program, encouraging drivers not to leave their engines running in drop-off and short-term parking areas. Mt. Bachelor also boasts an aggressive recycling program and requires all food and beverage suppliers to provide their environmental policies with each bid submitted.

> "Our commitment to Sundance has always been to develop very little and preserve a great deal."
> —Robert Redford, film director, actor, producer, and environmentalist

Squaw Valley USA, another Tahoe-area resort, utilizes energy exchange systems in several of its operations. The refrigeration system that freezes the ice-skating rink of the Olympic Ice Pavilion is a heat exchanger that simultaneously heats the Swimming Lagoon and Spa, as well as surrounding decks, walkways, and club. The twenty-eight-passenger Funitel, a gondola-type covered lift, utilizes heat from the lift's motors to warm the building via floor hydronics, while the cold air that is a by-product of the exchange system is recycled back to the engine room to cool the motors. In addition, Squaw Valley employs an incineration process to dispose of solid waste, which reduces landfill impact, and the heat generated is used to heat the Gold Coast, an upper-mountain lodge complex, reducing the need for fossil fuels.

Also at the forefront of the green movement in the ski industry is Sundance Resort in Utah. Well-known American actor, director, and producer Robert Redford purchased the small local ski area—then called Timphaven—in 1969 from the Stewart family when it consisted of only one chair lift, one rope tow, and a burger joint. Boldly ignoring advice from New York investors who envisioned a canyon full of lucrative hotels and condominiums, Redford dreamed of his new acquisition as a futuristic community model for environmental conservation and artistic experimentation. Sundance is now involved in numerous green initiatives. Examples include a linen reuse program, nontoxic cleaning supplies, natural products and organic soaps made in Sundance's Art Shack to stock the rooms, and an on-site resort-wide recycling program that includes turning glass bottles (via the resort's glass works kiln) into decorative art and housewares for use around the property.

> "A professor at Dartmouth's Thayer College of Engineering found that for every hour spent idling, a vehicle discharges 9.7 pounds of carbon emissions (diesel engines emit 19 pounds). Multiply that by the cars, buses and SUVs at most ski resorts and the carbon emissions add up!"
> —Mt. Bachelor website

It is impossible to mention all of the green practices being put into effect by all participating resorts; these are just a few of the more unique efforts being made. But the big question is this: what will be the motivating factor for *all* resorts to finally join wholeheartedly in the "go green" movement? If they wait until all that falls from the sky is rain, it will be too late. So we must help them with our influence.

The good news is that we *can* make a difference. And a big one. Resort areas will listen to us, the consumers, about our concerns, particularly when we vote with our tourist dollars. We can choose to frequent resorts where reversing the damage to our planet and caring for our earth is job one. We can find resorts that encourage our participation in the effort. It will take all of us engaged to make the changes that must be made to ensure there will be spiritual adventures in the snow for our children and grandchildren.

❄ A *Reflective Moment*

Take a few moments to reflect on how you might indulge your passion for snow play *and* help heal the earth at the same time. Here are a few ideas to get you started:

- *Leave no trace.* Whether in the backcountry or at a resort, employ a "leave no trace" philosophy. It likely goes without saying, but don't leave your trash for someone else, and if you encounter someone else's thoughtlessness, do something radical: pick it up and take it to the nearest receptacle. You'll feel great about having done a good deed (especially if you have to carry the trash down the mountain) and can smile about anonymously leaving the spot more pristine for the next adventurer.
- *Reduce your waste.* Cut down on the amount of trash you send to the landfill by choosing foods with the least amount of packaging. Use hand dryers in the restrooms rather than paper towels. Recycle and reuse everything that can be reused. Carry your own water in a reusable receptacle, use water fountains, or carry a collapsible cup to avoid escalating the mound of used paper cups—or do all of the above.
- *Reduce emissions.* Reduce your automobile emissions as much as possible. If you are vacationing and headed to a destination resort, don't rent a car unless you have to.

Many resorts have excellent public transportation and, when coupled with an airport shuttle to the resort, can be more than adequate. If you are local, carpool or use public transportation as much as possible. Don't leave your car running. After all, how much do you really need to pamper yourself? Have you really reached a point where you can't be cold for a few minutes while the engine heats up? To my way of thinking, a car shouldn't be run simply to warm it up unless the passenger is a newborn infant or other similarly fragile being. This is also a practice worth taking home!

- *Buy sustainable, green clothing and equipment when possible.* Ask your snow sports equipment and outdoor apparel retailers about green apparel and equipment, and encourage them to carry more of these items in their stores.
- *Be outspoken about recycling.* If you don't see tons of recycling receptacles in a resort area, bug folks about it! Ask the employees where the recycling bins are; ask to speak to management and tell them where more are needed. By the same token, if there are not recycling instructions with designated receptacles inside your lodging facility, even if it's just a hotel room, ask the manager to correct this situation.
- *Be heard with management.* If traveling with a group such as a ski club, a church group, or several families together, you carry clout with ski resorts. Groups are sought-after business, and repeat business is very highly valued. Ask to meet with the director of operations, and ask the director to share current resort policies and practices, as well as future plans, for being more earth-friendly. Express your concerns about what sustainable practices you are seeing or not seeing around the resort. Ask questions about responsible resort development and

expansion, how the resort sees itself addressing the problem of climate change, and whether the resort considers itself to be on the forefront of the green movement. You may be surprised to find that at many resorts, directors are accessible and eager to meet with the public. They appreciate having the opportunity to share what is a source of pride for them regarding their organization. These savvy directors know that, in a very competitive market, listening to the concerns of consumers is invaluable.

- *Do your research.* A good place to start is by visiting resort websites. Some resorts feature their sustainable philosophies and practices prominently on their home page. This sends the message that this issue is a high priority for both the resort management and the resort community. On other resort websites, trying to find the word "environment" or "green" amid all the words and graphics seeking to get you to part with your money seems nearly impossible. This too speaks volumes. The Ski Area Citizens Coalition uses a comprehensive point system to annually rate ski resorts according to their environmental policies and practices. Go to www.skiareacitizens.com for the top-ten list (and the bottom ten) and see how your favorite resort scored this year. Here are some sites that have information for finding ski resorts that are fully involved in green activities, beyond doing just enough for appearances:
  - ～ www.skiareacitizens.com
  - ～ www.nsaa.org/nsaa/environment/the_greenroom
  - ～ www.usatoday.com/travel/destinations/ski/2008-12-03-green-ski-resorts_N.htm
  - ～ www.usnews.com/blogs/fresh-greens/2009/1/5/where-to-find-the-best-and-worst-environmentally-friendly-ski-resorts.html

Conversation with an Adventurer

Tina Basich, U.S. snowboarding champion

❧

Tina Basich, women's snowboarding pioneer and a U.S. champion, is a founder of Boarding for Breast Cancer, a nonprofit youth-focused organization whose mission is education, awareness, and fund-raising. Tina was also instrumental in the growth of women's snowboarding when it was first evolving as a competitive sport. Here, she reflects on her experiences and the places where she left her mark.

What is it about snowboarding that makes it a spiritual adventure?

It's that feeling of being up on the mountain, especially in the backcountry, totally out there with Mother Nature doing something you're so passionate about. I always surrounded myself with friends, usually my brother and people I feel comfortable and safe with, because that's a huge deal. When all of those things come together, it's like the ride of your life. Everybody who has those things come together for them feels that high or that spirituality or that connection to the snow or to the mountains or to their friends. That is a lifelong, lasting feeling.

I think that's why so many of my friendships from snowboarding will last a lifetime, because when you go through adventures like that, you never forget them. Whenever we get together, we love retelling and reliving those stories because it was a *time*! We'll say, "Remember that time we were in the backcountry and the fog rolled in and the helicopter couldn't find us and we had to build a fire and almost spent the night in the woods?" And then, "Remember when you landed that first whatever, whatever?" I will reminisce about snowboarding for the rest of my life whether or not I have adventures like that ever again.

What is the result of all that joy and passion?

A feeling that is indescribable. Once people feel it, they can't just let it go. That's why people get hooked on snowboarding. People will quit their day jobs and wash dishes at night so they can go snowboard every day. All those elements, and all those feelings coming together, adrenaline or whatever it is rushing all around, create those moments we treasure so much. I remember saying to folks back in the day, "Be careful! You're gonna quit your day job if you come and ride with us." There is something about snowboarding that changes so many people's lives, people consistently say, "I tried snowboarding and never skied again!" or "I tried snowboarding and never went back to my day job!" or "I tried it and moved to Utah ..." It happens all the time. There is something that comes together and changes people. I think we have all the power in the world to create whatever we want for ourselves. So following our passion, our dreams, and making it happen is all in our hands.

How did you make your mark on the status of women in snowboarding?

I knew I was in this thing that was growing, and I was part of the beginning. I was part of helping women have a place in the sport, and we really got motivated. We developed one of the first women's snowboarding clothing lines, Shannon Dunn and I. We were pushing for women's products; we had some of the first women's pro-model snowboards designed especially for women riders. The whole thing became like a mission.

Can you share a story from that time?

One particular Big Air contest comes to mind, in 1994, in Innsbruck, Austria. There wasn't a women's division—we were there for another contest. My brother Mike was in the competition, and we went to the practice and were there checking out the jump, thinking maybe we could do it, and we were like, "No way, it's too big." Then the officials came right over to us and said, "No girls allowed." We were seriously probably not going to do it, but once they said no girls allowed, we were like, "Oh no, they didn't just say that! Oh, we're for sure going to do it now." So we went and got our boards and started hiking to the jump. They kept saying, "No women allowed." So we snuck up on the jump and dropped in. They came down and got us and said, "No, you can't do that." We said, "You have to let us go on. Give us one more practice run. If you think we are too dangerous, that's fine." So they gave us another practice run, and then they said, "Okay, you can be the demo event for the guys' competition." It was a night event, so we went home and got our pink outfits on and our pigtails and totally showed up. They were announcing us, saying, "Those crazy American girls are wanting to jump the jump!"

Some of the magazines later reported that we'd gone bigger than some of the guys that night and that we probably would have placed in the top ten. Those marks and the moments that we had, they changed everything. The next year that competition had a women's division. That was part of the longevity, too. We wanted to stay in it long enough to make our mark and leave our impression. I feel so lucky that I got to be a part of snowboarding in such a big way; it was such a big part of my life. Leaving my mark on snowboarding is rewarding to me; it was such a huge chapter of my life.

What happened that Boarding for Breast Cancer was born?

At first, it was, "Oh, my gosh! Our friend Monica is sick—we have to do something!" So we did something, we had a big event, and we donated money to foundations. That first year, in 1996, we had hoped to raise five thousand dollars, and we raised fifty thousand dollars. Then we realized that even that didn't completely fulfill our mission. Our friend died because she was misdiagnosed; she was told she was too young to have breast cancer. There was a lot of misinformation; the educational part was missing. It took us a couple of years of doing the Boarding for Breast Cancer events before we decided to turn ourselves into a nonprofit and develop our mission to educate women. Now we have traveling educational booths, and "early detection is best prevention" is our motto.

What has been the impact of Boarding for Breast Cancer?

Getting e-mails back from girls who discovered lumps after they learned how to do a self-breast exam in our booth. There've been so many people moved by what Boarding for Breast Cancer does. Young women have felt they have someone to turn to who's like them. It's not just handing them a brochure that has old ladies on it; it's not just our grandmas. It could be our best friends. We've had survivors who were twenty-three years old. It is amazing how many people are affected by breast cancer, and it's not only the person who has it, but it's the family and everyone around them.

What does it mean to you to have been a founder of such an important endeavor?

All that response from so many people who have been touched by Boarding for Breast Cancer has had a huge, huge impact on me, just knowing that we helped start something that affected somebody's life in a positive way like that. It means so much to me that we are able to accomplish that mission that all of us girls, including Monica, started. We didn't know it was going to be this big; we just felt like we had to do something. It has now turned into a big foundation that's worldwide. It's a go-to thing for a lot of young women, and they pass the word around. The message keeps going and going beyond our efforts. It's so rewarding. It's even better than that. I still get lots of e-mails and still respond to those e-mails. We have a whole awesome group of women who continue the work, and most of the original people are still involved with it.

⬧

Note to the reader: A portion of the authors' proceeds from this book are being donated to Boarding for Breast Cancer. If you would like to join us in helping this important cause, go to www.b4bc.org.

Epilogue

As we finish our journey of writing this book, spring is in full-fledged bloom here in Tahoe. The snow is melting on the runs of the now-closed resorts near our homes, and we've put our ski clothes in storage bins until next year. We each deal with "end of the season" letdown in different ways. Marcia has a timer on her cell phone that counts down the days until winter begins again. Karen ceremoniously hangs up her board in her garage and turns to tuning up her mountain bike. Of course, the consolation is the beauty of aspens budding out and the promise of long sunny days of hiking mountain vistas and rafting the Truckee River.

Having tuned-in to the spiritual adventures possible in the snow, we hope that when you've come to the close of your snowy escapades, whether that is at the dawn of spring or the end of a ski vacation, you will continue your journey of renewing your soul through the spiritual lessons learned on the slopes. We hope that the sheer fun and joy you discovered there will reverberate through your living and lift your spirits. We pray that your renewed passion will spur something surprising for you that continues to give you that "woo-hoo" feeling. And we trust that the connection you have to the Divine Love that runs a course through all of creation will give you not only peace but also a yearning for more. More adventures. More spirit. More soulful renewal. And, of course, more snow in your future!

A Week of Meditations
for Spiritual Adventures
in the Snow

What follows are meditations based on themes from this book. We invite you to explore these experiential exercises as a way of bringing a heightened spiritual perspective to your snow adventures. If you are on the mountain for a one-week vacation, you might want to use one each day. If you have only a few days, select those that appeal to you. If you are blessed to be a local, consider designating some of your days on the slopes as a time to intentionally raise the level of your experience with these spiritual reflections. Then come up with some of your own as you continue your endeavor to be a spiritual adventurer.

Day 1—First Things First

Find a majestic spot where you can be still for a few moments. If you have been here before, pretend for a moment that you are on the mountain for the very first time. Allow your senses to become intoxicated with the plethora of incoming stimuli. Isolate them one by one to heighten your awareness. First, let your eyes drink in beauty. Marvel at the contours of the mountains. If it is snowing, look up and be mesmerized by following a few snowflakes to the ground one at a time. Take in the color of the sky, the asymmetry of trees. Take a few moments to inundate your eyes with all that you observe.

Next, close your eyes for a moment. What do you hear? Can you identify each noise? Are there voices? The sound of the machinery cranking the lift? Skis and boards on snow? Now, listen more closely for more subtle sounds. Can you hear wind in the trees? Bird chatter?

Turn your attention now to your sense of smell. What does your nose know? Does the air tell of an approaching snowstorm? Can you smell the pungent fragrance of pine? The woodsy smell of other trees?

Tilting your face to the sky, open your mouth and taste the snowflakes for a few moments. (If it is not snowing, find a patch of clean snow and have a taste.) Let your childlike wonder run rampant.

Open your eyes and take off a glove (only briefly, if temperatures are frigid). Pick up some snow and rub it between your fingers. Hold it in your hand. Touch the bark of a tree. Feel the uneven texture.

Allow your senses to be overwhelmed by taking in all of these amazing stimuli at once. Have that for yourself for an instant and hold precious this moment in time. Fathom the Great Imagination, the Creative Genius, and the blessing of your good fortune to be the beneficiary of it all. Continue to hold the intention to really notice all that your senses take in; watch how your awareness grows. Carry this gift with you into your snow adventures.

Day 2—A New Altitude Attitude

Think of your run down the mountain (and, if applicable, your ride back up) as a journey or pilgrimage. On a slope or trail that you can comfortably ski or board, use your rhythm to facilitate an experience of "letting go." With each turn (or step, if snowshoeing; or each stride or push, if cross country skiing), envision letting go of some things you no longer need. These may be negative thoughts or patterns that no longer serve you, old emotions, stresses, tensions, conflicts, guilts. Let go of anything that holds you back and weighs you down. Imagine hearing each one go "plop" in the snow behind you.

After doing this for a period of time, you will begin to feel lighter and more energized. When this occurs, shift your focus to entering a state of gratitude. A natural time to make the shift may be when starting a new trail or heading back up on the lift. Let your eyes fall on the sky, trees, mountain, and so on, and with each new thing you see, offer the words, "Thank you" or "I am grateful." Then turn your focus to your body. Become aware of your toes, feet, ankles, calves, knees, thighs, and so on. Experience gratitude for the wonder of you, you who are able to exhilarate in this awesome adventure.

Day 3—Mix It Up

Today is a day for becoming more aware of your body as a conduit for spiritual experience. First, tune in to what is your usual manner of descending the slope. What is your particular groove? Do you "point and shoot," flying top to bottom with no stops, your gaze fixed only on the terrain ahead? Do you measure your day by how many runs made at breakneck speed? Or do you make long loopy turns, taking your time as if out for a leisurely stroll, savoring the scenery and observing the other folks on the hill? Or does your groove lie somewhere in between?

For a few runs today, intentionally and drastically change up your groove. If you are a speed demon, take a few meandering runs. Notice the deep green of the trees, the different textures of tree bark, the intense color of the sky. Notice the others of your species out enjoying the day. Take note of your legs, your knees, your toes. Feel what your muscles need to do to keep you upright. Feel their movement, their contractions, and their weight shift at the edge of balance.

If you are a gentle meanderer, ski or ride with more intention. Be bold. Be passionate. Go for it. Be aware of what it feels like in your body to raise the level of adrenaline. Notice your heart rate and pay attention to your breathing. Let your fear or nervousness translate into excitement. Find the edges of your balance. Become aware of how you are holding your back, your shoulders. Feel the amazing muscles in your feet, calves, and thighs.

Now stop completely and take a few deep breaths. Reflect on the experience of mixing it up. Do you see any applications to real life? Skiing and riding can be a great laboratory for testing out changes you might want to try on for a bit.

Then relax and go back to your groove with a new level of awareness.

Day 4—The Trail Map of Your Life

One of the most exciting (and scary) spiritual adventures is the one that happens in the undiscovered trail map of our inner selves. It's important to know what the terrain is like. Are there mountains of self-doubt heaped up inside that need to be conquered? Perhaps you feel quagmired in negativity in a relationship, as if you were stuck up to your waist in fresh powder. Is the avalanche danger level high as you feel the pressure of things at work come crashing down faster than you can keep up?

Get a trail map from your favorite ski resort or cross country area. Then sit down with a pen or pencil and begin to imagine that this is the geography of your life. Write words that come to you related to each part of the map. For instance, what is "home base" (the lodge, the village) in your life? What grounds you? Where or who is it that gives you the feeling of home? Go to the summit and write those things that bring you "mountaintop" feelings. Then name each of the runs with a situation in your life. Green ones—beginner runs—can become metaphors for what in your life is filled with ease, where you can just flow. (Or, depending on your perspective and your ability level, the green runs may be things in your life that you find ordinary, mundane, boring, or a means to getting somewhere else.) Blue intermediate runs may be a little more challenging. They may require only a little effort at times but contain unexpected steep points or a few bumps along the way. What parts of your life fit blue terrain? Finally, where are you encountering the double black diamonds in your life? What is the most challenging thing you are facing? What feels the most risky? Is there anything that terrifies you?

Now take a look at your "life trail" map. Consider which areas of the terrain you want or need to explore further. Are you staying too long in the safe confines of home base or beginner runs and feel a need to venture out more in your life? How might you take on the occasional challenges offered by the blue runs of your life with a new attitude or new energy? What would it be like to feel the fear associated with the expert runs of your life and do them anyway?

As you travel different runs today, feel in your body and notice in your spirit how you approach and ski or ride these different parts of the mountain. What can you learn from the ways you ski or ride these different runs that would help you with the corresponding areas of your life?

Day 5—Asking a Question

In her book on walking a labyrinth, *Walking a Sacred Path: Rediscovering the Labyrinth as a Spiritual Tool*, Lauren Artress describes one way of preparing for a walk as "Asking a Question." She explains that most of us carry around questions and search for clues to the puzzles of life, often not realizing we are doing it. Bringing that search to your conscious mind before a run on the slopes can open you to transforming your stuck questions to a place of movement, moving them from unanswered to some form of insight.

Preparation for this exercise can happen before you get to the mountain, before you get to the top of the slope or beginning of the trail. The first step is to name one question you are wrestling with. You may want to write this in a journal for yourself, or you may want to add accountability to the exercise and share that question with someone else. Your question may be about a decision you are trying to make, a burden that is weighing you down, or something more general, such as, "What is it that I need to focus on right now to bring greater satisfaction/love/peace to my life?"

The next step is to give yourself permission to shut out the million other things that might be crowding your mind. Consider this as a gift to your spirit—the luxury of being about only this one thing right now. Nothing else has to matter at this moment. Sometimes a deep breath can help calm your thoughts and energy. If praying is a practice for you, this is the time for a prayer of preparation that can be as simple as "Open me to possibilities."

Then head out. Just be open. Don't worry about whether or not the "answers" will come. Just live with the question(s). Your easy focus on these matters for the day, or just one run, will move *something* in your spirit as your body moves with the rhythm of the run.

Day 6—Be a Meaning Monger

We are "meaning mongers." As human beings, our brains are wired to deal in the exchange of experience and meaning. We have an ability to create meaningful associations with just about anything we encounter. Today's meditation is about going through the day looking for metaphors.

For instance, as you put on your first layer of clothing, let your thoughts search for the people or things in your life that keep you warm, that protect you. As you don your jacket and snow pants, notice their color or pattern. Do they reflect something about you? Bright and loud, perhaps, or subtle and calm? What kind of energy would you like to put out into the world today?

When you put on your helmet, let that lead you to reflecting on what boundaries you have created or need to create to protect yourself, and what boundaries are limiting you. Are you hardheaded sometimes? Do you need to soften the barriers to let in new ideas and experiences? Or do you frequently feel wounded by others? Do you need a little "thicker skin" to deal with some people or situations in your life?

Continue in this frame of mind as you deal with your equipment: "What are the areas of my life that are weighing me down like these heavy skis I'm carrying right now?" or "Do I have the right equipment for the terrain of my life that I'm navigating right now?" Perhaps getting your skis or board waxed will remind you that taking time to prepare spiritually in difficult situations can help you glide through the sticky stuff.

You are probably seeing how being a meaning monger works. We do it all the time without thinking about it, actually. Today, just turn up the dial and see what insights happen.

Day 7—Taking It Home

This meditation is good for ending your ski trip (or season) on a high note by turning "last-day blues" into gratitude and taking it all with you. Begin by reflecting on what stands out as the most memorable moments of the week (or season).

Which runs were your favorites? Where did you have a breakthrough of finding your groove? Where did you stop and savor mountaintop beauty? What was most meaningful? Where did your sense of wonder come alive? Were you awestruck? When did you have a moment that you wanted never to end? What about those moments where you felt challenged?

Reflect on these times. Then go back and relive some of these moments by skiing or riding some of those same runs again. Allow your gratitude to flow through you as you carve turns. Savor your favorite and most meaningful experiences one more time. Align them in your body and in your memory in such a way that you can call them to mind easily, even when you are far from the mountain. Gently determine to leave in the snow those things that would be best left behind (Judgment? Defensiveness? Worry? Procrastination?). Sail down the mountain claiming a new beginning. Delight in taking your inner spiritual adventurer home with you.

How to Talk Cool on the Mountain: A Guide to Slope Slang

To get you in the mood for your spiritual adventures in the snow, we thought you might need a "primer" of terms so you can be über-cool on the slopes. Even if you are a veteran on the snow, the slang keeps morphing and changing. We certainly hadn't heard of all of these before we began this project! Here are some of our favorite need-to-know bits of information:

bake sale: Groomer lingo for snow condition that exists when lots of frozen snow cookies form on the surface of the snow and insist on hanging around. See also **cookies**.

the big "ahhhhh": The sound you make back at the car when freeing your feet from ski boots. Known as "the best feeling in the world" at that moment.

black ice: The unfortunate occurrence of water, usually runoff from melted snow, freezing on black asphalt. It is treacherous because, blending in with the blacktop, it cannot be seen. Black ice can form from runoff on even the sunniest days and can lead to some quite gnarly traffic accidents.

blowin' smoke: The glorious experience of skiing in powder so fine that it blows up like smoke behind the rider.

bluebird day: Gorgeous, sunny day with great snow, when the bluebird of happiness lights on your shoulder. (We hope that's all she does.)

bluebird skier: Snow adventurer who will only ski, of course, on bluebird days. However, a contradiction in terms exists: the bluebird skier does not necessarily relish a bluebird *powder* day.

Instead, skiing on perfect corduroy is what constitutes a bluebird skier's perfect bluebird day.

box: A human-made feature in a terrain park that is box-shaped (duh!) and is usually raised just above the level of the snow. It has a slick surface (most are about 18 inches wide and 10–15 inches long), making it easy to slide across on board or skis.

brat pack: Young folks who run in packs and are oblivious to anyone else's presence. They may crowd you out on the lift, stomp all over your board or skis (without so much as a "sorry" or "'scuse me"), cut you off, and mow you over. They may smoke even on the lift with you without so much as a "ya mind?" and leave their butts in the snow. If you are reading this and see yourself, go ask your mama for a redo on the manners lessons. Karen recently watched one of these in a lift line as he grabbed the chair in front, allowing it to pull him into place to wait for the next chair, an activity strongly discouraged by lifties. The chaired slowed right where it always does, and the kid whacked his head on the safety bar … hard. Karen believes in karma, so she tried to suppress her laughter. It should go without saying, but we will point out that not all young folks are brat-packers. In fact, many more are nice, friendly, fun to meet, and very cool to hang and ride with. If you see yourself *here*, go thank your mama.

bring your snorkel: Your reply when your buddy calls you on the slopes to ask how deep the pow-pow is. This is the kind of day many of us would leave our jobs for (and many do).

bummer: When you drop a glove or cell phone from the ski lift. See also **major bummer**.

snowcat: Not the feline kind. (We've never seen a puss in ski boots, anyway.) These are the grooming machines (apparently whether or not they are made by Caterpillar—probably most of them used to be and the name stuck) that work at night to tame the hacked-up snow into deliriously dreamy corduroy. See also **corduroy**.

chain monkeys: The guys (sorry, but so far in our experience it really is all guys—if someone sees a woman chain monkey, we would love to know about it!) in bright yellow rainsuits who, while you are en route to your favorite mountain during a winter storm, will relieve you of thirty dollars to put your chains on your flatlander car. If you get caught without chains, you can purchase them from the monkeys for another fifty dollars. It's another fifteen dollars for the chain monkeys to take them off. Cha-ching! Never leave home without your chains—or a wad of cash.

chairhog: Skiers/boarders who go to great lengths (including elbows, generally taking up lots of space) to make sure only they and a buddy or two wind up on the approaching chair, even when there are lift lines. These hogs clearly have never been to ski lift etiquette school and do not know how to alternate from the different lines feeding the chair.

cidiot: Combination of the words "city" and "idiot." Applies to those who travel (usually driving) from large cities to ski areas. No further explanation needed. Hopefully, we will be forgiven the smile that spreads across our face when we spy the red pickup—which just passed us on a two-lane road as if we were standing still—now stuck in a snowbank after having experienced a spinout. See also **flatlander; spinout**.

cleanup on aisle 6: Groomer lingo for a stubborn situation on a slope, such as ruts, ridges, tracks, or other messes that require another snowcat to come through and clean up the mess.

cookies: Large granules that continuously freeze and refreeze, becoming larger and larger so as to be the size of cookies. This makes for some difficult and unpleasant conditions. On most days, we would rather ski and ride on solid ice than on cookies. See also **bake sale**.

corduroy: Resembling corduroy fabric, the delicious occurrence of fresh powder perfectly groomed into those endless one-inch rows of pure bliss. We genuflect to the snowcats and their humans who miraculously create such paradise.

corn: Occurs mostly in the spring, when the combination of repetitive melting and refreezing conditions (accompanied by grooming) creates small granules. Early in the day when still frozen, its characteristic clatter and intense vibration sound and feel like skiing on gravel, and we wonder about long-term damage to the teeth. However, spring corn (natural, not groomed) is what many backcountry skiers live for. It is at its best in the middle of the day during its "melt" phase and is usually only perfect—really soft and smooth—for only a few hours. Backcountry skiers go out in search of six-thousand-foot descents on corn!

death by cookies: Not an après-ski activity in which one consumes way too many warm, fresh-from-the-oven chocolate chip delights. Rather, a painful fall due to large cookie-sized granules that make it challenging to stay upright in the turns. See also **cookies**.

diehards: The adventurers on the mountain in blizzard conditions with seventy-five-mile-an-hour winds and no visibility. Can't see your hand in front of your face? Can't tell up from down because of complete whiteout? When everyone else has left the area, and when the resort finally closes due to high winds and otherwise unsafe conditions, the diehards are the last ones off the mountain. When a blizzard has closed highways and the highway patrol is asking folks to stay put and off the roads, the diehards are driving to their next adventure in their 4WDs.

dippin' dots day: When the snow coming down is really closer to hail and bounces like birdshot pellets off your helmet. The name comes from the fact that it looks like the new ice-cream craze that's in the same shape. Cover every bit of exposed skin to avoid pain.

dust on crust: Snow condition resulting from less than an inch of snow that has fallen on frozen hardpack.

feet cast in concrete: What the crossover skier experiences when trying snowboarding for the first time. Skiers are accustomed to being able to move their feet independently of each other, a feat impossible in snowboarding. See also **three days of pain**.

flatlander: Frequent visitor to the mountains who has enough sense and savvy in the snow to be a local, but just happens to live down the hill "in the flats."

French fries: It may seem that ski instructors are subliminally trying to increase food sales in the ski lodge. In actuality, when instructors ask little ski bunnies to make French fries, they are teaching them how make parallel turns. See also **pizza**.

freshies: Fresh snow in any amount bringing delight to the avid snow adventurer, as in, "Gotta get out in the freshies!"

getting plowed: Being in the wrong place at the wrong time, as the object of a collision with an out-of-control skier or snowboarder. (Skier's code requires that the skier behind watch out for the skier in front.)

gnar: Snow in any of its forms making skiing and riding possible. See also **schralping the gnar**.

gnarl: The primal growling sound you make when you are schralping, going for it, adrenaline pumping, with utmost gusto.

gnarly: Unfavorable to really bad. Sometimes shortened to gnar, as in, "That's some gnar gnar, dude!" Translation: "Look out for the nasty conditions, chump!"

groomers: Runs where the snowcats have tamed the carved-up pow-pow once more into corduroy bliss. See also **corduroy**.

hoodie: What you wear under your helmet to keep your head and face from freezing off. *Haute couture* of bank robbers. If someone who thinks they are more cool tells you they are just as warm in a bandana, they are lying.

jib: Bonking, scraping across, and otherwise having close encounters with rails, boxes, tabletops, logs, and other terrain park features with one or two sticks on your feet. It seems as if the word might have been co-opted from the sports of sailing and windsurfing, because it is so similar to the word "jibe," which means "turning upwind," but the connection is not immediately apparent.

jonesing: A deep, gnawing craving to be ripping it up on the mountain so as to capture a natural high. Usually a malady that runs rampant as fall days turn colder and grayer. Side effects include a stiff neck as the afflicted crane their necks, searching the sky above.

liftie: Your friend who is working so you can be whisked away back to the top of the mountain in pursuit of euphoria. Smile and say "hi" and "thanks" when you load. (At first glance, this may not appear to be hard work, but watch for a while as they keep the loading area snow-covered and level, not to mention the literally hundreds of kids they lift onto the chair in a given shift.)

lift ticket: A.k.a. liability release. *What? My lift ticket is a liability release?* You betcha. Most state something to the effect that "as a condition of being permitted to use the ski area premises, facilities, and equipment, I agree to release, hold harmless, and indemnify [whatever resort], their parent companies,"... blah, blah, blah ... "on my own behalf and on behalf of" my offspring and other greedy family members, "from any and ALL CLAIMS for personal injury, death, or property damage, including those caused by the NEGLIGENCE" of all those crazy people on the mountain. As if that's not enough, "I agree to assume all risks associated with skiing, snowboarding, tubing, other recreational activities, and the use of lifts" and pretty much everything else under the sun. Some add, "If you are unwilling to accept the inherent risks and the skier's responsibility as outlined in the ... Skier Safety Act, return this ticket UNUSED and UNATTACHED for a full refund." Yeah, right! Any stats available on how many folks have done that?

line: The distance between two points that in skiing/riding is a somewhat imaginary (until accomplished) linking of point A (top of slope) to point B (bottom of slope). Used most often in backcountry and extreme skiing lingo, where finding a descendible line may well ensure your survival. The translation of this to resort skiing is when you are wanting to yell, "Pick a line!" to the rather unpredictable skier/rider in front of you, the driving equivalent of which is, of course, "Pick a lane!"

major bummer: When you drop a glove or cell phone from the ski lift into an area that you would never attempt to ride or ski if your life depended on it. Major-bummer realization sets in at the moment you watch your phone disappear into the hole it makes in three feet of soft powder. As the chair is swiftly moving away, you look around for landmarks to point out the spot, only to notice the thousands of other small holes all around that are keeping your phone company.

mardi gras tree: An unassuming tree that, through no fault of its own, has become the collector of an assortment of colorful beads tossed by snow adventure revelers when they pass next to it on the lift. Extra points are awarded if said beads are tossed during the actual Mardi Gras week. At some resorts, the flung-to-be-hung items of choice are not beads but various undergarments, which adorn the unsuspecting tree.

mercy pass: Groomer lingo for one single ribbon of groomed 'roy cut into acres of powder on a cherished run. This usually happens when so much white has dumped through the night that groomers cut only a single swath down many of the runs— partly due to time constraints, partly to gift us with so much glorious untracked powder. Shredders and skiers jump in and out of the swath to glory in the freshies. A hilarious sight is when the pow-pow is so deep, riders and skiers get stuck and fall all along the edges till so many folks are lying all along the swath it looks like someone went bowling with human pins. See also **freshies; pow-pow; 'roy**.

park: Terrain park where all sorts of terrain features are built into the slope for jibbing, including boxes, tabletops, logs, rails, and jumps. See also **jib; terrain park**.

park rat: Skiers and snowboarders who prefer to spend most of their time in the terrain park, bouncing off of natural and human-crafted features. See also **rat pack**.

pizza: When ski instructors encourage a small kid to make a pizza, they are not actually expecting the little tyke to pull some dough and pepperoni out of his/her coat pockets to ease some snowplay-induced hunger pangs. Instructors are teaching him/her to snowplow by making the shape of a slice of pizza with his/her skis. See also **French fries**.

point 'n shoot: Formerly a type of camera, this is now a type of skiing/riding in which you point your stick(s) downhill and shoot for the bottom, no turns necessary.

pole pal: On a snowcat track, road, or other flat expanse of trail, just at the moment that a snowboarder knows that he/she must pop out of a binding to access that propulsion power known as skating, a serendipitous event occurs in an exceptionally cool skier who happens by and extends a pole for a quick crack-the-whip- style pull. This gives the snowboarder just enough momentum to traverse until the next slight slope without popping out. It is way cool to board with a ski buddy who manages to be there offering the pole at just the right time. It is even cooler to be offered a pole by a stranger who is just an exceptional person. Thanks, pole pals! This happened to Karen recently when a young teenager extended a pole to her. "Just at the moment when I thought she would give me a pull, she let the pole go, meaning for me to use it myself on the flat. I had actually never done it quite like that before. Perhaps this is how the sport of paddle boarding in water was invented! She was very sweet and said she helped her brother like that all the time. Of course, then I had to find her at the bottom to give her her pole back, but still, it was a very nice gesture."

powder hound: Adventurer whose love of playing in pow-pow exceeds reasonable proportions. It would not be entirely unlikely or extremely unusual that a powder hound would kiss a perfectly good job goodbye for a day in exceptional powder. See also **pow-pow**.

pow-pow: Light, fluffy snow. When held in your hand, you can blow it away like baby powder. It doesn't make snowballs or snowmen. Best when delivered by a storm that requires measurement in feet rather than inches.

rail: A terrain park feature named for its shape and size resembling a handrail.

rat pack: A group of park rats who frequent the parks but can sometimes be found having a great time cruising other runs. They are generally less obnoxious and more respectful of others and of the environment than brat packs. See also **brat pack**.

rooster tail: Blowin' smoke with such symmetry that consecutive arcs hang high in the air from perfectly executed turns. When watching this from downslope on a bluebird day, the sun shining through the smoke and giving the appearance of twinkling stars in the daytime, there is no doubt that heaven is right here on earth. Co-opted from jet-skiing. See also **blowin' smoke; bluebird day**.

'roy: Short slang for corduroy. See **corduroy**.

schralping: Originally a surfing term that means facing down a challenge, adrenaline pounding, going for it with huge gusto.

schralping the gnar: Going for it big in any kind of snow.

serious major bummer: When the chair lift is covered with ice and you disembark from the lift with not only a frozen fanny but also your pants sticking to the chair. As you disembark, "RRRRRIIIIP!" That's right … horror of horrors, part of your pants stays on the chair, stuck to the ice. AAAARRRRGGGGGGHHH! But there's always a bright side. Go show yourself to Guest Services, and you just might score a free lift ticket or a new pair of pants, or both—depending on how full the moon is!

shredding: It isn't enough just to ride that snowboard, you see. Shredding means you are tearing up the terrain, carving intensely with your "shred sled." Not necessarily something you do on the bunny hill.

Sierra cement: Heavy wet snow that occasionally falls in the Sierra and other places. It makes great snowballs and snowmen and, when knocked from your board, falls with a resounding "thud." An interesting fact about Sierra cement is that with expert resort groomers at the ready, second-day Sierra cement is every bit as dreamy as pow-pow on the groomed runs. See also **pow-pow**.

skins: A brilliant piece of equipment that, when stretched over the bottom of your skis, creates traction, allowing you to hike uphill on said skis.

slope hog: The rider who is zigzagging unpredictably all over the entire run, to whom you have the irresistible urge to yell, "Pick a line!" See also **line**.

smoke: On a grand day of pow-pow, the fine residue of powder that hangs in the air as evidence of a snow adventurer making turns. See also **blowin' smoke; pow-pow**.

snow envy: Because there is no commandment that specifically states, "Thou shalt not covet thy neighbor's snow," this is your condition when the particular mountain range where you live or frequent is having a less-than-optimal year of snowfall. And every time you hear anything about those "other" resort areas, they are, of course, experiencing storms of epic proportions, blanketing them in record amounts of white bliss. See also **supreme snow envy**.

spinout: What happens when cidiots, flatlanders, weekend wallies, and even locals become overzealous to reach the slopes. The vehicle spins out of control, coming to rest off the road. Most spunout vehicles could not be considered "off-road" worthy. See also **cidiot; weekend wally**.

stick(s): Your snowboard equals one stick; your skis are … well … two.

supreme snow envy: A variation of snow envy that occurs when you have just dropped thousands of dollars on a ski vacation with lousy to mediocre snow conditions, only to have the epic storm move in on the day you are flying out. See also **snow envy**.

terrain park: Where the forty-somethings and older are hoping all the adolescent skiers/riders will go. And where the adolescent riders are hoping the forty-somethings and older won't go. Karen's five-year-old loves it so much it is already the only place he wants to ski, only he thinks it is called the "train" park.

three days of pain: What beginning snowboarders must go through in order to begin having a blast on a snowboard. Beginning snowboarders spend quite a bit of time on their fannies and on their knees. Falls that impact the hands and wrists can also be brutal. Hence, a relatively new phenomenon in the sport available to beginners: fanny pads, padded snowboarding pants, knee pads, and wrist guards available for sale and rental. Once these three days are survived, it is generally agreed that the subsequent learning curve toward a degree of proficiency is shorter than with learning to ski. See also **feet cast in concrete**.

trail map: The rather innocent-looking piece of paper on which your destiny is laid out in oh-so-cheery colors, and about which you may want to enroll in the tutorial "How to Refold Your Trail Map Back to Pocket-Size without Looking Like a Goon." This may be your first clue to wondering just what you have gotten yourself into when you discover runs with names like Pucker Face, Lier's Slide, and Doom and Gloom. Taken literally, how do you feel about launching yourself down Drop-off, The Plunge, Surprise, or Widowmaker? How about O. God? What do you suppose they mean by Ballhooter?

vanity fall: The inevitable wipeout that happens as you ski under the lift saying to yourself, "I sure do look good." This is also known as "funny as all heck" to the people watching you from the lift.

weekend wally: The snow adventurer who frequents the ski areas on weekends. Usually courteous, but not prone to large amounts of common sense around snow, driving, and other related logistical concerns. If you see a vehicle with a mound of snow on top (poised to fall down onto the windshield or to be launched onto the windshield of the unsuspecting car behind), it must be a weekend wally. See also **cidiot; flatlander**.

yard sale: The result of a spectacular fall when your equipment and apparel are scattered far and wide as if to display goggles, gloves, skis, poles, cell phone, and so on for sale.

Suggestions for
Further Reading

Basich, Tina. *Pretty Good for a Girl: The Autobiography of a Snowboarding Pioneer*. With Kathleen Gasperini. New York: HarperCollins, 2003.

Boyd, Johnny. *First Tracks*. Snowmass Village, CO: PTO Press, 2008.

Chickerneo, Nancy Barrett. *Woman Spirit Awakening in Nature: Growing Into the Fullness of Who You Are*. Woodstock, VT: SkyLight Paths, 2008.

Comins, Mike. *A Wild Faith: Jewish Ways into Wilderness, Wilderness Ways into Judaism*. Woodstock, VT: Jewish Lights, 2007.

Gallwey, Timothy W., and Robert Kriegel. *Inner Skiing*. New York: Random House, 1997.

Jones, Melanie Davis. *I Can Ski*. Danbury, CT: Children's Press, 2004.

Korngold, Jamie. *God in the Wilderness: Rediscovering the Spirituality of the Great Outdoors with the Adventure Rabbi*. New York: Doubleday, 2008.

Lamott, Anne. *Grace (Eventually): Thoughts on Faith*. New York: Riverhead Trade, 2008.

Lionberger, John. *Renewal in the Wilderness: A Spiritual Guide to Connecting with God in the Natural World*. Woodstock, VT: SkyLight Paths, 2007.

McGee, Margaret D. *Sacred Attention: A Spiritual Practice for Finding God in the Moment*. Woodstock, VT: SkyLight Paths, 2007.

Phipps, Rick. *Skiing Zen: Searching for the Spirituality of Sport*. Tucson, AZ: Iceni Books, 2006.

Schmidt, Gary, and Susan M. Felch. *Winter: A Spiritual Biography of the Season.* Woodstock, VT: SkyLight Paths, 2003.

Sing, Susan Saint. *Spirituality of Sport: Balancing Body and Soul.* Cincinnati, OH: Saint Anthony Messenger Press, 2004.

A Word from the Authors

We invite you to continue your spiritual adventures in the snow by checking out more resources at our website: www.spiritualadventuresinthesnow.com. In writing this book, we had so much fun interviewing people, both famous and not so famous, that we've decided to continue this part of our adventure. On our website you'll find more interviews, as well as fun links to some of the people, events, and references we've mentioned in this book.

You'll also find information on our downloadable companion workbooks that you can use for your personal reflections or as a way of having some structured conversations and experiences together as a group. The workbooks come in various formats, some using the inclusive spiritual language we've used in this book and others with a Christian perspective for church youth or adult groups. If you plan to come to Tahoe to ski any of our wonderful resorts, you can invite us to be with your group for a day, an evening, or the duration of your trip. Find out how to reach us for this purpose on our website. Our site also offers links to ski experiences led by spiritual adventurers in the Jewish tradition and the practice of Zen.

A portion of the author proceeds of this book are going to two organizations with which we have become connected through the writing of this book. You read about the nonprofit pioneered by Tina Basich and friends, Boarding for Breast Cancer, in the "Conversation with an Adventurer" at the end of chapter 8. And we were so inspired by adaptive snowboarder

Evan Strong (see the "Conversation with an Adventurer" at the end of chapter 7), as well as other adaptive skiers and snowboarders, that we are also donating a portion of our proceeds to Disabled Sports USA Far West. Both of these organizations are doing amazing, life-changing work. If you'd like to join in supporting them, you can donate through the links on www.spiritualadventuresinthesnow.com.

Spirituality & Crafts

Beading—The Creative Spirit
Finding Your Sacred Center through the Art of Beadwork
by Rev. Wendy Ellsworth
Invites you on a spiritual pilgrimage into the kaleidoscope world of glass and color.
7 x 9, 240 pp, 8-page full-color insert, plus b/w photographs and diagrams
Quality PB, 978-1-59473-267-6 **$18.99**

Contemplative Crochet
A Hands-On Guide for Interlocking Faith and Craft
by Cindy Crandall-Frazier; Foreword by Linda Skolnik
Illuminates the spiritual lessons you can learn through crocheting.
7 x 9, 208 pp, b/w photographs, Quality PB, 978-1-59473-238-6 **$16.99**

The Knitting Way
A Guide to Spiritual Self-Discovery
by Linda Skolnik and Janice MacDaniels
Examines how you can explore and strengthen your spiritual life through knitting.
7 x 9, 240 pp, b/w photographs, Quality PB, 978-1-59473-079-5 **$16.99**

The Painting Path
Embodying Spiritual Discovery through Yoga, Brush and Color
by Linda Novick; Foreword by Richard Segalman
Explores the divine connection you can experience through creativity.
7 x 9, 208 pp, 8-page full-color insert, plus b/w photographs
Quality PB, 978-1-59473-226-3 **$18.99**

The Quilting Path
A Guide to Spiritual Discovery through Fabric, Thread and Kabbalah
by Louise Silk
Explores how to cultivate personal growth through quilt making.
7 x 9, 192 pp, b/w photographs and illustrations, Quality PB, 978-1-59473-206-5 **$16.99**

The Scrapbooking Journey
A Hands-On Guide to Spiritual Discovery
by Cory Richardson-Lauve; Foreword by Stacy Julian
Reveals how this craft can become a practice used to deepen and shape your life.
7 x 9, 176 pp, 8-page full-color insert, plus b/w photographs
Quality PB, 978-1-59473-216-4 **$18.99**

The Soulwork of Clay
A Hands-On Approach to Spirituality
by Marjory Zoet Bankson; Photographs by Peter Bankson
Takes you through the seven-step process of making clay into a pot, drawing parallels at each stage to the process of spiritual growth.
7 x 9, 192 pp, b/w photographs, Quality PB, 978-1-59473-249-2 **$16.99**

Or phone, fax, mail or e-mail to: SKYLIGHT PATHS Publishing
Sunset Farm Offices, Route 4 • P.O. Box 237 • Woodstock, Vermont 05091
Tel: (802) 457-4000 • Fax: (802) 457-4004 • www.skylightpaths.com
Credit card orders: **(800) 962-4544** (8:30AM–5:30PM ET Monday–Friday)
Generous discounts on quantity orders. SATISFACTION GUARANTEED. Prices subject to change.

Spiritual Biography / Reference

Hearing the Call across Traditions
Readings on Faith and Service
Edited by Adam Davis; Foreword by Eboo Patel
Explores the connections between faith, service, and social justice through the prose, verse, and sacred texts of the world's great faith traditions.
6 x 9, 352 pp, HC, 978-1-59473-264-5 **$29.99**

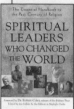

Spiritual Leaders Who Changed the World
The Essential Handbook to the Past Century of Religion
Edited by Ira Rifkin and the Editors at SkyLight Paths; Foreword by Dr. Robert Coles
An invaluable reference to the most important spiritual leaders of the past 100 years.
6 x 9, 304 pp, 15+ b/w photos, Quality PB, 978-1-59473-241-6 **$18.99**

Spiritual Biography—SkyLight Lives

SkyLight Lives reintroduces the lives and works of key spiritual figures of our time—people who by their teaching or example have challenged our assumptions about spirituality and have caused us to look at it in new ways.

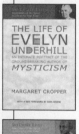

The Life of Evelyn Underhill
An Intimate Portrait of the Groundbreaking Author of Mysticism
by Margaret Cropper; Foreword by Dana Greene
Evelyn Underhill was a passionate writer and teacher who wrote elegantly on mysticism, worship, and devotional life.
6 x 9, 288 pp, 5 b/w photos, Quality PB, 978-1-893361-70-6 **$18.95**

Mahatma Gandhi: His Life and Ideas
by Charles F. Andrews; Foreword by Dr. Arun Gandhi
Examines from a contemporary Christian activist's point of view the religious ideas and political dynamics that influenced the birth of the peaceful resistance movement.
6 x 9, 336 pp, 5 b/w photos, Quality PB, 978-1-893361-89-8 **$18.95**

Simone Weil: A Modern Pilgrimage
by Robert Coles
The extraordinary life of the spiritual philosopher who's been called both saint and madwoman.
6 x 9, 208 pp, Quality PB, 978-1-893361-34-8 **$16.95**

Zen Effects: The Life of Alan Watts
by Monica Furlong
Through his widely popular books and lectures, Alan Watts (1915–1973) did more to introduce Eastern philosophy and religion to Western minds than any figure before or since.
6 x 9, 264 pp, Quality PB, 978-1-893361-32-4 **$16.95**

More Spiritual Biography

Bede Griffiths: An Introduction to His Interspiritual Thought
by Wayne Teasdale
The first study of his contemplative experience and thought, exploring the intersection of Hinduism and Christianity.
6 x 9, 288 pp, Quality PB, 978-1-893361-77-5 **$18.95**

The Soul of the Story: Meetings with Remarkable People
by Rabbi David Zeller
Inspiring and entertaining, this compelling collection of spiritual adventures assures us that no spiritual lesson truly learned is ever lost.
6 x 9, 288 pp, HC, 978-1-58023-272-2 **$21.99**
(A book from Jewish Lights, SkyLight Paths' sister imprint)

Spirituality of the Seasons

Autumn: A Spiritual Biography of the Season
Edited by Gary Schmidt and Susan M. Felch; Illustrations by Mary Azarian
Rejoice in autumn as a time of preparation and reflection. Includes Wendell Berry, David James Duncan, Robert Frost, A. Bartlett Giamatti, E. B. White, P. D. James, Julian of Norwich, Garret Keizer, Tracy Kidder, Anne Lamott, May Sarton.
6 x 9, 320 pp, 5 b/w illus., Quality PB, 978-1-59473-118-1 **$18.99**

Spring: A Spiritual Biography of the Season
Edited by Gary Schmidt and Susan M. Felch; Illustrations by Mary Azarian
Explore the gentle unfurling of spring and reflect on how nature celebrates rebirth and renewal. Includes Jane Kenyon, Lucy Larcom, Harry Thurston, Nathaniel Hawthorne, Noel Perrin, Annie Dillard, Martha Ballard, Barbara Kingsolver, Dorothy Wordsworth, Donald Hall, David Brill, Lionel Basney, Isak Dinesen, Paul Laurence Dunbar. 6 x 9, 352 pp, 6 b/w illus., Quality PB, 978-1-59473-246-1 **$18.99**

Summer: A Spiritual Biography of the Season
Edited by Gary Schmidt and Susan M. Felch; Illustrations by Barry Moser
"A sumptuous banquet.... These selections lift up an exquisite wholeness found within an everyday sophistication."— ★ *Publishers Weekly* starred review
Includes Anne Lamott, Luci Shaw, Ray Bradbury, Richard Selzer, Thomas Lynch, Walt Whitman, Carl Sandburg, Sherman Alexie, Madeleine L'Engle, Jamaica Kincaid.
6 x 9, 304 pp, 5 b/w illus., Quality PB, 978-1-59473-183-9 **$18.99**
HC, 978-1-59473-083-2 **$21.99**

Winter: A Spiritual Biography of the Season
Edited by Gary Schmidt and Susan M. Felch; Illustrations by Barry Moser
"This outstanding anthology features top-flight nature and spirituality writers on the fierce, inexorable season of winter.... Remarkably lively and warm, despite the icy subject." — ★ *Publishers Weekly* starred review
Includes Will Campbell, Rachel Carson, Annie Dillard, Donald Hall, Ron Hansen, Jane Kenyon, Jamaica Kincaid, Barry Lopez, Kathleen Norris, John Updike, E. B. White.
6 x 9, 288 pp, 6 b/w illus., Deluxe PB w/flaps, 978-1-893361-92-8 **$18.95**

Spirituality / Animal Companions

Blessing the Animals: Prayers and Ceremonies to Celebrate God's Creatures, Wild and Tame *Edited by Lynn L. Caruso*
5¼ x 7¼, 256 pp, Quality PB, 978-1-59473-253-9 **$15.99**; HC, 978-1-59473-145-7 **$19.99**

Remembering My Pet: A Kid's Own Spiritual Workbook for When a Pet Dies
by Nechama Liss-Levinson, PhD, and Rev. Molly Phinney Baskette, MDiv; Foreword by Lynn L. Caruso
8 x 10, 48 pp, 2-color text, HC, 978-1-59473-221-3 **$16.99**

What Animals Can Teach Us about Spirituality: Inspiring Lessons from Wild and Tame Creatures *by Diana L. Guerrero* 6 x 9, 176 pp, Quality PB, 978-1-893361-84-3 **$16.95**

Spirituality—A Week Inside

Come and Sit: A Week Inside Meditation Centers
by Marcia Z. Nelson; Foreword by Wayne Teasdale
6 x 9, 224 pp, b/w photos, Quality PB, 978-1-893361-35-5 **$16.95**

Lighting the Lamp of Wisdom: A Week Inside a Yoga Ashram
by John Ittner; Foreword by Dr. David Frawley
6 x 9, 192 pp, 10+ b/w photos, Quality PB, 978-1-893361-52-2 **$15.95**

Making a Heart for God: A Week Inside a Catholic Monastery
by Dianne Aprile; Foreword by Brother Patrick Hart, OCSO
6 x 9, 224 pp, b/w photos, Quality PB, 978-1-893361-49-2 **$16.95**

Waking Up: A Week Inside a Zen Monastery
by Jack Maguire; Foreword by John Daido Loori, Roshi
6 x 9, 224 pp, b/w photos, Quality PB, 978-1-893361-55-3 **$16.95**; HC, 978-1-893361-13-3 **$21.95**

Spirituality

Claiming Earth as Common Ground: The Ecological Crisis through the Lens of Faith *by Andrea Cohen-Kiener; Foreword by Rev. Sally Bingham*
Inspires us to work across denominational lines in order to fulfill our sacred imperative to care for God's creation. 6 x 9, 192 pp, Quality PB, 978-1-59473-261-4 **$16.99**

The Losses of Our Lives: The Sacred Gifts of Renewal in Everyday Loss
by Dr. Nancy Copeland-Payton
Reframes loss from the perspective that our everyday losses help us learn what we need to handle the major losses. 6 x 9, 176 pp (est), HC, 978-1-59473-271-3 **$19.99**

The Workplace and Spirituality: New Perspectives on Research and Practice *Edited by Dr. Joan Marques, Dr. Satinder Dhiman and Dr. Richard King*
Explores the benefits of workplace spirituality in making work more meaningful and rewarding. 6 x 9, 256 pp, HC, 978-1-59473-260-7 **$29.99**

A Spirituality for Brokenness: Discovering Your Deepest Self in Difficult Times *by Terry Taylor*
Guides you through a compassionate yet highly practical process of facing, accepting, and finally integrating your brokenness into your life—a process that can ultimately bring mending. 6 x 9, 176 pp, Quality PB, 978-1-59473-229-4 **$16.99**

Next to Godliness: Finding the Sacred in Housekeeping
Edited and with Introductions by Alice Peck
Offers new perspectives on how we can reach out for the Divine.
6 x 9, 224 pp, Quality PB, 978-1-59473-214-0 **$19.99**

Bread, Body, Spirit: Finding the Sacred in Food
Edited and with Introductions by Alice Peck
Explores how food feeds our faith. 6 x 9, 224 pp, Quality PB, 978-1-59473-242-3 **$19.99**

Renewal in the Wilderness: A Spiritual Guide to Connecting with God in the Natural World *by John Lionberger*
Reveals the power of experiencing God's presence in many variations of the natural world. 6 x 9, 176 pp, b/w photos, Quality PB, 978-1-59473-219-5 **$16.99**

Honoring Motherhood: Prayers, Ceremonies and Blessings
Edited and with Introductions by Lynn L. Caruso
Journey through the seasons of motherhood. 5 x 7¼, 272 pp, HC, 978-1-59473-239-3 **$19.99**

Soul Fire: Accessing Your Creativity *by Rev. Thomas Ryan, CSP*
Learn to cultivate your creative spirit. 6 x 9, 160 pp, Quality PB, 978-1-59473-243-0 **$16.99**

Money and the Way of Wisdom: Insights from the Book of Proverbs
by Timothy J. Sandoval, PhD 6 x 9, 192 pp, Quality PB, 978-1-59473-245-4 **$16.99**

Creating a Spiritual Retirement: A Guide to the Unseen Possibilities in Our Lives
by Molly Srode 6 x 9, 208 pp, b/w photos, Quality PB, 978-1-59473-050-4 **$14.99**
HC, 978-1-893361-75-1 **$19.95**

Finding Hope: Cultivating God's Gift of a Hopeful Spirit
by Marcia Ford 8 x 8, 200 pp, Quality PB, 978-1-59473-211-9 **$16.99**

Jewish Spirituality: A Brief Introduction for Christians *by Lawrence Kushner*
5½ x 8½, 112 pp, Quality PB, 978-1-58023-150-3 **$12.95** *(A book from Jewish Lights, SkyLight Paths' sister imprint)*

Journeys of Simplicity: Traveling Light with Thomas Merton, Bashō, Edward Abbey, Annie Dillard & Others *by Philip Harnden*
5 x 7¼, 144 pp, Quality PB, 978-1-59473-181-5 **$12.99**; 128 pp, HC, 978-1-893361-76-8 **$16.95**

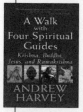

Keeping Spiritual Balance As We Grow Older: More than 65 Creative Ways to Use Purpose, Prayer, and the Power of Spirit to Build a Meaningful Retirement
by Molly and Bernie Srode 8 x 8, 224 pp, Quality PB, 978-1-59473-042-9 **$16.99**

Spiritually Incorrect: Finding God in All the *Wrong* Places *by Dan Wakefield; Illus. by Marian DelVecchio* 5½ x 8½, 192 pp, b/w illus., Quality PB, 978-1-59473-137-2 **$15.99**

A Walk with Four Spiritual Guides: Krishna, Buddha, Jesus, and Ramakrishna
by Andrew Harvey 5½ x 8½, 192 pp, 10 b/w photos & illus., Quality PB, 978-1-59473-138-9 **$15.99**

Spiritual Practice

Haiku—The Sacred Art: A Spiritual Practice in Three Lines
by Margaret D. McGee Introduces haiku as a simple and effective way of tapping into the sacred moments that permeate everyday living.
5½ x 8½, 192 pp, Quality PB, 978-1-59473-269-0 **$16.99**

Dance—The Sacred Art: The Joy of Movement as a Spiritual Practice
by Cynthia Winton-Henry Invites all of us, regardless of experience, into the possibility of dance/movement as a spiritual practice.
5½ x 8½, 224 pp, Quality PB, 978-1-59473-268-3 **$16.99**

Spiritual Adventures in the Snow: Skiing & Snowboarding as Renewal for Your Soul *by Dr. Marcia McFee and Rev. Karen Foster; Foreword by Paul Arthur* Explores snow sports as tangible experiences of the spiritual essence of our bodies and the earth. 5½ x 8½, 208 pp, Quality PB, 978-1-59473-270-6 **$16.99**

Recovery—The Sacred Art: The Twelve Steps as Spiritual Practice
by Rami Shapiro; Foreword by Joan Borysenko, PhD Uniquely interprets the Twelve Steps of Alcoholics Anonymous to speak to everyone seeking a freer and more God-centered life. 5½ x 8½, 240 pp, Quality PB, 978-1-59473-259-1 **$16.99**

Soul Fire: Accessing Your Creativity *by Rev. Thomas Ryan, CSP*
Shows you how to cultivate your creative spirit as a way to encourage personal growth.
6 x 9, 160 pp, Quality PB, 978-1-59473-243-0 **$16.99**

Running—The Sacred Art: Preparing to Practice
by Dr. Warren A. Kay; Foreword by Kristin Armstrong Examines how your daily run can enrich your spiritual life. 5½ x 8½, 160 pp, Quality PB, 978-1-59473-227-0 **$16.99**

Hospitality—The Sacred Art: Discovering the Hidden Spiritual Power of Invitation and Welcome *by Rev. Nanette Sawyer; Foreword by Rev. Dirk Ficca*
5½ x 8½, 192 pp, Quality PB, 978-1-59473-228-7 **$16.99**

Thanking & Blessing—The Sacred Art: Spiritual Vitality through Gratefulness
by Jay Marshall, PhD; Foreword by Philip Gulley 5½ x 8½, 176 pp, Quality PB, 978-1-59473-231-7 **$16.99**

Everyday Herbs in Spiritual Life: A Guide to Many Practices
by Michael J. Caduto; Foreword by Rosemary Gladstar
7 x 9, 208 pp, 21 b/w illustrations, Quality PB, 978-1-59473-174-7 **$16.99**

Divining the Body: Reclaim the Holiness of Your Physical Self *by Jan Phillips*
8 x 8, 256 pp, Quality PB, 978-1-59473-080-1 **$16.99**

The Gospel of Thomas: A Guidebook for Spiritual Practice
by Ron Miller; Translations by Stevan Davies 6 x 9, 160 pp, Quality PB, 978-1-59473-047-4 **$14.99**

Labyrinths from the Outside In: Walking to Spiritual Insight—A Beginner's Guide
by Donna Schaper and Carole Ann Camp
6 x 9, 208 pp, b/w illus. and photos, Quality PB, 978-1-893361-18-8 **$16.95**

Practicing the Sacred Art of Listening: A Guide to Enrich Your Relationships and Kindle Your Spiritual Life *by Kay Lindahl* 8 x 8, 176 pp, Quality PB, 978-1-893361-85-0 **$16.95**

The Sacred Art of Bowing: Preparing to Practice
by Andi Young 5½ x 8½, 128 pp, b/w illus., Quality PB, 978-1-893361-82-9 **$14.95**

The Sacred Art of Chant: Preparing to Practice
by Ana Hernández 5½ x 8½, 192 pp, Quality PB, 978-1-59473-036-8 **$15.99**

The Sacred Art of Fasting: Preparing to Practice
by Thomas Ryan, CSP 5½ x 8½, 192 pp, Quality PB, 978-1-59473-078-8 **$15.99**

The Sacred Art of Forgiveness: Forgiving Ourselves and Others through God's Grace
by Marcia Ford 8 x 8, 176 pp, Quality PB, 978-1-59473-175-4 **$16.99**

The Sacred Art of Listening: Forty Reflections for Cultivating a Spiritual Practice
by Kay Lindahl; Illustrations by Amy Schnapper
8 x 8, 160 pp, b/w illus., Quality PB, 978-1-893361-44-7 **$16.99**

The Sacred Art of Lovingkindness: Preparing to Practice
by Rabbi Rami Shapiro; Foreword by Marcia Ford 5½ x 8½, 176 pp, Quality PB, 978-1-59473-151-8 **$16.99**

Sacred Speech: A Practical Guide for Keeping Spirit in Your Speech
by Rev. Donna Schaper 6 x 9, 176 pp, Quality PB, 978-1-59473-068-9 **$15.99**
HC, 978-1-893361-74-4 **$21.95**

About SKYLIGHT PATHS Publishing

SkyLight Paths Publishing is creating a place where people of different spiritual traditions come together for challenge and inspiration, a place where we can help each other understand the mystery that lies at the heart of our existence.

Through spirituality, our religious beliefs are increasingly becoming a part of our lives—rather than *apart* from our lives. While many of us may be more interested than ever in spiritual growth, we may be less firmly planted in traditional religion. Yet, we do want to deepen our relationship to the sacred, to learn from our own as well as from other faith traditions, and to practice in new ways.

SkyLight Paths sees both believers and seekers as a community that increasingly transcends traditional boundaries of religion and denomination—people wanting to learn from each other, *walking together, finding the way.*

For your information and convenience, at the back of this book we have provided a list of other SkyLight Paths books you might find interesting and useful. They cover the following subjects:

Buddhism / Zen	Global Spiritual	Monasticism
Catholicism	Perspectives	Mysticism
Children's Books	Gnosticism	Poetry
Christianity	Hinduism /	Prayer
Comparative	Vedanta	Religious Etiquette
Religion	Inspiration	Retirement
Current Events	Islam / Sufism	Spiritual Biography
Earth-Based	Judaism	Spiritual Direction
Spirituality	Kabbalah	Spirituality
Enneagram	Meditation	Women's Interest
	Midrash Fiction	Worship

Or phone, fax, mail or e-mail to: SKYLIGHT PATHS Publishing
Sunset Farm Offices, Route 4 • P.O. Box 237 • Woodstock, Vermont 05091
Tel: (802) 457-4000 • Fax: (802) 457-4004 • www.skylightpaths.com
Credit card orders: (800) 962-4544 (8:30AM–5:30PM ET Monday–Friday)
Generous discounts on quantity orders. SATISFACTION GUARANTEED. Prices subject to change.

**For more information about each book,
visit our website at www.skylightpaths.com**